THIS BOOK BELONGS TO

The Library of

....

....

I can't tell you how grateful I am that you decided to read my book. My most heartfelt thanks that you took time out of your life to choose my work and I hope you find benefit within these pages.

There are so many books available today that offer similar content so that makes it even more humbling that you decided to buying mine.

Tell me what you thought! I am eager to hear your opinion and ideas on what you read as are others who are looking for a good book to buy. Leave a review on Amazon.com so others can benefit from your wisdom!

With much thanks.

Table of Contents

Chapter 1 – Tools of the trade   30

Chapter 2 – Shading and Color Play   34

Chapter 3 - The Head and face   39

Chapter 4 A study of the human head and face   47

Chapter 5 - A Study of the Lips   57

Chapter 6 – A Study of the Nose   63

Chapter 7 – The Study of the Arm   70

Chapter 8 - A Study of the Leg   80

Chapter 9 - A Study of the Female Figure   91

Chapter 10 - A Study of the Male Form   111

Final Words   129

SUMMARY

Mastering human figure drawing is of great significance for several reasons. Firstly, it allows artists to accurately depict the human form in their artwork. The human figure is one of the most complex and beautiful subjects to draw, and being able to capture its proportions, anatomy, and movement is essential for creating realistic and compelling artwork.

Secondly, mastering human figure drawing provides a solid foundation for artists to explore other areas of art, such as portraiture, character design, and even sculpture. Understanding the human figure allows artists to accurately portray the unique features and expressions of individuals, bringing their artwork to life and creating a deeper connection with the viewer.

Furthermore, human figure drawing is not only important for traditional artists but also for those working in digital art and animation. In these mediums, the ability to draw the human figure accurately is crucial for creating believable and dynamic characters. Whether it's designing a character for a video game or animating a scene in a movie, having a strong understanding of human figure drawing allows artists to create characters that are visually appealing and relatable to the audience.

Moreover, mastering human figure drawing also enhances an artist's ability to express emotions and tell stories through their artwork. The human figure is capable of conveying a wide range of emotions through body language, facial expressions, and gestures. By mastering human figure drawing, artists can effectively communicate their intended message and evoke specific emotions in their audience.

Additionally, mastering human figure drawing can also improve an artist's observational skills. Drawing the human figure requires careful observation of proportions, angles, and details. This attention to detail and observation can be applied to other aspects of an artist's work, allowing them to better capture the essence of their subject matter, whether it be landscapes, still life, or abstract concepts.

Lastly, mastering human figure drawing can also serve as a form of self-expression and personal growth. The process of studying and practicing human figure drawing allows artists to explore their own artistic style and develop their unique voice. It provides a platform for self-reflection and self-discovery, as artists learn to express their thoughts, emotions, and experiences through their artwork.

In conclusion, mastering human figure drawing is of great significance for artists as it enables them to accurately depict the human form, explore other areas of art, enhance their ability to express emotions and tell stories, improve their observational skills, and serve as a form of self-expression and personal growth. It is a fundamental skill that lays the groundwork for creating compelling and impactful artwork.

The essential drawing tools encompass a wide range of materials and instruments that are indispensable for any artist or aspiring artist. These tools are crucial for creating stunning and visually captivating artworks, whether it be for sketching, painting, or any other form of artistic expression.

One of the most fundamental drawing tools is a pencil. Pencils come in various grades, ranging from soft to hard, and each grade offers a different level of darkness and texture. Artists often use different grades of pencils to achieve various effects and to add depth and dimension to their drawings. Pencils are versatile and can be used for sketching, shading, and creating intricate details.

Another essential drawing tool is a set of high-quality erasers. Erasers are crucial for correcting mistakes and refining details in a drawing. There are different types of erasers available, such as kneaded erasers, which can be molded into different shapes to erase small areas or create highlights, and vinyl erasers, which are more suitable for erasing larger areas.

In addition to pencils and erasers, artists also rely on a variety of pens and markers. Fine-tip pens are ideal for creating precise lines and intricate details, while markers offer vibrant and bold colors. These tools are commonly used for inking and adding vibrant colors to drawings. Artists often use different types of pens and markers, such as brush pens, technical pens, and alcohol-based markers, to achieve different effects and textures.

Paintbrushes are another essential tool for artists, particularly those who work with watercolors, acrylics, or oils. Paintbrushes come in various shapes and sizes, each designed for specific techniques and applications. Flat brushes are ideal for covering large areas, while round brushes are perfect for creating fine details and intricate lines. The choice of paintbrushes depends on the artist's preferred style and the desired effect.

Furthermore, a drawing board or easel is essential for providing a stable surface to work on. These tools allow artists to position their artwork at a comfortable angle and height, enabling them to work with ease and precision. Drawing boards and easels come in different sizes and designs, catering to the specific needs and preferences of artists.

Lastly, a sketchbook or drawing pad is a must-have for any artist. These provide a dedicated space for artists to practice their skills, experiment with different techniques, and record their ideas and inspirations.

A line drawing refers to a simplified representation of an object or scene using only lines. It typically focuses on the outlines and essential features of the subject, omitting details such as shading or texture. Line drawings are often used in various artistic disciplines, such as illustration, graphic design, and animation, as well as in technical fields like architecture and engineering.

Contour drawing, on the other hand, is a specific technique within line drawing that involves creating an outline that follows the contours or edges of the subject. It aims to capture the three-dimensional form and structure of the object or scene by carefully observing and tracing its visible edges. Contour drawings can be done with various drawing tools, such as pencils, pens, or markers, and can be executed in a variety of styles, ranging from precise and detailed to loose and expressive.

Both line drawing and contour drawing are fundamental techniques in the visual arts, serving as a foundation for more complex and detailed renderings. They allow artists to simplify complex subjects, emphasize important elements, and convey a sense of form and volume. These techniques are often used as initial sketches or studies before creating more refined and polished artworks.

Line drawings and contour drawings can be created using different approaches and methods. Some artists prefer to work directly from observation, carefully studying the subject and translating its visual characteristics onto paper. Others may rely on reference photographs or their imagination to create line drawings and contour drawings. Regardless of the approach, these techniques require a keen eye for observation, an understanding of form and proportion, and a mastery of various drawing techniques, such as hatching, cross-hatching, and stippling.

In addition to their artistic applications, line drawings and contour drawings also have practical uses. In technical fields, line drawings are often used to communicate ideas, concepts, or designs in a clear and concise manner. Architects, engineers, and product designers, for example, use line drawings to illustrate plans, elevations, and sections of buildings or objects. These drawings help convey important information about dimensions, proportions, and spatial relationships.

In conclusion, line drawing and contour drawing are essential techniques in the visual arts and have practical applications in various fields. They allow artists to simplify complex subjects, emphasize form and structure, and communicate ideas effectively. Whether used for artistic expression or technical communication, these techniques require skill, observation, and a deep understanding of the subject matter.

Portrait composition and framing are crucial elements in photography that can greatly impact the overall aesthetic and storytelling of an image.

When it comes to capturing a portrait, the composition refers to how the various elements within the frame are arranged and organized. It involves making deliberate choices about the placement and positioning of the subject, as well as considering the background, foreground, and any other elements that may be present.

One of the key aspects of portrait composition is the rule of thirds. This rule suggests that the frame should be divided into nine equal parts by two equally spaced horizontal lines and two equally spaced vertical lines. The subject should then be placed along these lines or at the points where they intersect. This technique helps to create a visually pleasing and balanced composition, as it avoids placing the subject directly in the center of the frame, which can often result in a static and less engaging image.

Another important consideration in portrait composition is the use of leading lines. These are lines within the frame that guide the viewer's eye towards the subject or other important elements in the image. Leading lines can be created by various elements such as roads, fences, or even the natural contours of the landscape. By incorporating leading lines into the composition, the photographer can create a sense of depth and visual interest, as well as draw attention to the subject.

Framing, on the other hand, refers to how the subject is enclosed or surrounded within the frame. It involves carefully selecting the boundaries of the image and considering what elements should be included or excluded. The choice of framing can greatly influence the mood and narrative of the portrait. For example, a tight close-up framing can create a sense of intimacy and focus solely on the subject's facial expressions, while a wider framing can provide context and show the subject within their environment.

In addition to composition and framing, other factors such as lighting, posing, and background also play a significant role in portrait photography. The lighting can enhance the mood and highlight certain features of the subject, while the posing can convey a particular emotion or message. The background, whether it is blurred or in focus, can either complement or contrast with the subject, adding depth and visual interest to the image.

Overall, portrait composition and framing are essential skills for any photographer aiming to capture compelling and visually appealing portraits. By carefully considering the placement of the subject, utilizing leading lines, and making deliberate choices about framing, photographers can create images that not only showcase the subject but also tell a story and evoke emotions in the viewer.

Building a body from basic shapes involves the process of creating a human or animal figure using simple geometric forms as a foundation. This technique is commonly used in various art forms, such as drawing, painting, sculpture, and even digital design.

To begin with, the artist or designer starts by visualizing the desired pose or stance of the body. This mental image serves as a guide throughout the construction process. The basic shapes used typically include circles, ovals, rectangles, and triangles, which are combined and manipulated to form the different parts of the body.

The head is often represented by a circle or an oval shape, which serves as the starting point for facial features and hair. The torso is usually constructed using a rectangular shape, which can be elongated or shortened depending on the desired proportions. The limbs, such as arms and legs, are commonly represented by elongated rectangles or cylinders, which can be bent or twisted to create dynamic poses.

Once the basic shapes are in place, the artist or designer can then refine and add details to the body. This involves adding more specific shapes to represent features such as hands, feet, and facial features. For example, the hands can be represented by smaller ovals or rectangles, while the feet can be depicted using triangular shapes.

The next step in the process is to add volume and depth to the body. This is achieved by adding shading and highlights to the different shapes, creating the illusion of three-dimensionality. Shadows are typically added to areas that are not directly exposed to light, while highlights are added to areas that catch the light source.

Furthermore, the artist or designer can also add texture and surface details to the body. This can be done by adding lines, dots, or patterns to represent clothing, skin texture, or other surface characteristics. These details help to enhance the realism and overall visual appeal of the body.

Building a body from basic shapes requires a good understanding of anatomy and proportions. It is important to study and observe the human or animal form in order to accurately represent it using simple geometric forms. Practice and experimentation are also key in developing this skill, as it takes time and effort to master the art of constructing a body from basic shapes.

In conclusion, building a body from basic shapes is a fundamental technique used in various art forms. It involves visualizing and constructing the body using simple geometric forms, refining and adding details, and creating volume and depth through shading and highlights.

Designing compelling compositions is a crucial aspect of any creative project. Whether it's a website, a poster, a magazine layout, or even a painting, the composition plays a significant role in capturing the viewer's attention and conveying the intended message effectively.

To create a compelling composition, one must consider various elements such as balance, contrast, hierarchy, and unity. These elements work together to create a visually pleasing and harmonious arrangement of elements within the design.

Balance is a fundamental principle in composition. It refers to the distribution of visual weight within a design. There are two types of balance: symmetrical and asymmetrical. Symmetrical balance involves arranging elements equally on both sides of a central axis, creating a sense of stability and formality. On the other hand, asymmetrical balance involves arranging elements of different sizes, shapes, and colors in a way that creates a sense of equilibrium through visual weight distribution.

Contrast is another crucial element in composition. It involves using differences in color, size, shape, texture, or value to create visual interest and make certain elements stand out. Contrast helps guide the viewer's eye and adds depth and dimension to the design.

Hierarchy is essential in guiding the viewer's attention and conveying the intended message effectively. It involves organizing elements in a way that establishes a clear visual order. This can be achieved through the use of size, color, placement, or typography. By establishing a hierarchy, the designer can emphasize important elements and create a sense of flow and structure within the composition.

Unity is the principle that brings all the elements of a composition together. It involves creating a sense of harmony and coherence by ensuring that all the elements work together as a whole. This can be achieved through the use of consistent colors, fonts, and styles, as well as through repetition and alignment.

In addition to these elements, designers must also consider the overall mood and emotion they want to evoke through their composition. This can be achieved through the use of color psychology, typography, and imagery. By carefully selecting and arranging these elements, designers can create compositions that evoke specific emotions and resonate with the intended audience.

Overall, designing compelling compositions requires a thoughtful and strategic approach. By considering elements such as balance, contrast, hierarchy, unity, and emotion, designers can create visually appealing and impactful compositions that effectively communicate their message.

Developing a personal style is a process that involves exploring and experimenting with different fashion choices, accessories, and grooming techniques to create a unique and authentic look that reflects your personality and individuality. It is a way of expressing yourself and making a statement without saying a word.

One of the first steps in developing a personal style is to understand your own preferences and tastes. Take some time to reflect on what you like and dislike in terms of clothing, colors, patterns, and overall aesthetics. Consider the types of outfits that make you feel confident and comfortable, as well as the ones that make you feel self-conscious or out of place. This self-awareness will serve as a foundation for building your personal style.

Next, it's important to gather inspiration from various sources. Look to fashion magazines, social media influencers, celebrities, and even street style for ideas and inspiration. Pay attention to the details that catch your eye, such as unique accessories, interesting combinations of colors and textures, or unexpected pairings of different clothing styles. However, it's crucial to remember that while inspiration is valuable, it should not be copied blindly. Instead, use it as a starting point to develop your own interpretation and twist.

Experimentation is key when it comes to developing a personal style. Don't be afraid to try new things and step out of your comfort zone. Visit different stores and boutiques, both online and offline, to explore a wide range of options. Try on different styles of clothing, mix and match different pieces, and experiment with different hairstyles and makeup looks. This process of trial and error will help you discover what works best for you and what doesn't.

Another important aspect of developing a personal style is understanding your body type and dressing accordingly. Different body types have different proportions and features that can be accentuated or minimized through clothing choices. Learn about your body shape and identify the styles and silhouettes that flatter your figure the most. This will help you make informed decisions when shopping and ensure that you feel confident and comfortable in your outfits.

Building a personal style also involves paying attention to the small details. Accessories, such as jewelry, belts, scarves, and hats, can add a unique touch to your outfits and help you stand out. Experiment with different accessories to find the ones that complement your personal style and add that extra flair to your overall look.

Digital drawing is a form of art that utilizes digital tools and software to create illustrations, paintings, and other visual artworks. It has gained popularity in recent years due to its convenience, versatility, and the wide range of creative possibilities it offers.

One of the main advantages of digital drawing is the ability to work on a digital canvas, which eliminates the need for physical materials such as paper, paint, and brushes. This not only saves costs but also reduces waste and clutter. Additionally, digital drawing allows for easy editing and undoing mistakes, as well as the ability to experiment with different techniques and styles without fear of ruining the artwork.

Digital drawing also offers a wide range of tools and features that can enhance the creative process. These include various brushes, pens, and pencils that can mimic traditional art tools, as well as the ability to adjust opacity, size, and pressure sensitivity. This allows artists to achieve a level of precision and control that may be difficult to achieve with traditional mediums.

Furthermore, digital drawing provides the opportunity to work with layers, which are essentially transparent sheets that can be stacked on top of each other. This allows artists to separate different elements of their artwork, making it easier to make changes and adjustments without affecting the rest of the composition. Layers also enable artists to experiment with different effects and textures, as well as create depth and dimension in their artwork.

Another advantage of digital drawing is the ability to easily share and distribute artwork. With the rise of social media platforms and online art communities, artists can showcase their work to a global audience, receive feedback, and connect with other artists. Digital files can also be easily reproduced and printed, allowing artists to sell their work as prints or merchandise.

In terms of accessibility, digital drawing has made art more inclusive and accessible to a wider range of people. Traditional art supplies can be expensive and may require a certain level of skill to use effectively. However, with digital drawing, all that is needed is a computer or tablet and a drawing software, which are more affordable and easier to learn. This has opened up opportunities for aspiring artists who may not have had access to traditional art supplies or formal art education.

In conclusion, digital drawing offers numerous advantages and opportunities for artists. It provides a convenient and versatile platform for creating artwork, with a wide range of tools and features that enhance the creative process. It also allows for easy editing, experimentation, and sharing of artwork.

Preparing for exhibitions and art school applications involves a comprehensive and meticulous approach to showcasing one's artistic abilities and potential. It requires careful planning, organization, and attention to detail in order to effectively present one's work and stand out among a competitive pool of applicants.

To begin with, preparing for exhibitions involves selecting the right pieces of artwork that best represent one's artistic style and vision. This requires a critical evaluation of one's portfolio, considering factors such as the quality of the artwork, its relevance to the theme or concept of the exhibition, and its potential to captivate and engage viewers. It is important to curate a cohesive body of work that demonstrates technical skill, creativity, and a unique artistic voice.

In addition to selecting the artwork, it is crucial to prepare the physical presentation of the pieces. This includes framing or mounting the artwork in a professional and aesthetically pleasing manner. Attention should be given to the choice of materials, colors, and textures that complement the artwork and enhance its visual impact. Proper labeling and documentation of the artwork, including titles, dimensions, and medium, is also essential for exhibition purposes.

Furthermore, preparing for art school applications requires a thoughtful and strategic approach. It is important to research and identify the specific requirements and expectations of each art school to which one is applying. This may include submitting a portfolio of artwork, writing an artist statement, providing letters of recommendation, and completing application forms. Each component of the application should be carefully crafted to highlight one's strengths, achievements, and potential as an artist.

When assembling a portfolio for art school applications, it is important to showcase a diverse range of artistic skills and techniques. This may include drawings, paintings, sculptures, digital art, or any other medium that demonstrates versatility and adaptability. The portfolio should also reflect a strong conceptual understanding and the ability to communicate ideas effectively through visual means.

Additionally, writing an artist statement is a crucial component of art school applications. This statement should provide insight into one's artistic process, inspirations, and intentions. It should articulate a clear artistic vision and demonstrate critical thinking skills. The artist statement should be concise, well-written, and reflective of one's unique artistic voice.

Lastly, securing strong letters of recommendation from art teachers, mentors, or professionals in the field can greatly enhance one's art school application. These letters should highlight one's artistic abilities, work ethic, and potential for growth.

Finding inspiration and motivation for drawing can be a challenging task, especially when you feel stuck or lacking creative energy. However, there are several strategies and techniques that can help you overcome this hurdle and reignite your passion for art.

One effective way to find inspiration is by exploring different art styles and techniques. Take the time to study the works of renowned artists, both past and present, and analyze their unique approaches to drawing. This can expose you to new ideas and perspectives, and may even inspire you to experiment with different styles in your own work.

Another way to find motivation is by immersing yourself in the art community. Attend local art exhibitions, workshops, and classes to connect with fellow artists and gain exposure to different artistic perspectives. Engaging in conversations with other artists can spark new ideas and provide valuable feedback on your own work.

Additionally, seeking inspiration from nature can be a powerful source of motivation. Take walks in scenic locations, observe the beauty of the natural world, and try to capture its essence through your drawings. Whether it's the intricate patterns of a leaf or the vibrant colors of a sunset, nature offers endless inspiration for artists.

Furthermore, setting goals and creating a routine can help you stay motivated and focused on your drawing practice. Establish specific objectives, such as completing a certain number of drawings per week or mastering a particular technique, and track your progress. Breaking down larger goals into smaller, achievable tasks can make the creative process more manageable and rewarding.

Lastly, don't be afraid to take breaks and allow yourself time to recharge. Sometimes, stepping away from your artwork for a while can actually enhance your creativity and provide a fresh perspective when you return. Engage in activities that you enjoy outside of drawing, such as reading, listening to music, or practicing mindfulness, as these can help clear your mind and rejuvenate your artistic spirit.

In conclusion, finding inspiration and motivation for drawing is a personal journey that requires exploration, engagement, and self-reflection. By exposing yourself to different art styles, connecting with the art community, seeking inspiration from nature, setting goals, and taking breaks when needed, you can overcome creative blocks and reignite your passion for drawing. Remember, the key is to stay curious, open-minded, and persistent in your artistic pursuits.

As an artist, it is crucial to continuously explore and delve into the intricacies of the human form. The human body is an endless source of inspiration, offering a multitude of shapes, sizes, and proportions that can be endlessly studied and interpreted. By immersing oneself in the exploration of the human form, artists can not only enhance their technical skills but also deepen their understanding of the human experience.

One of the primary reasons why artists should keep exploring the human form is the sheer beauty and complexity it possesses. The human body is a masterpiece of nature, with its curves, lines, and contours creating a visually captivating subject. By studying and capturing the human form, artists can develop a keen eye for detail, honing their ability to observe and replicate the intricacies of the human body in their artwork.

Moreover, exploring the human form allows artists to tap into the emotional and psychological aspects of the human experience. The body is a vessel that carries our emotions, thoughts, and experiences, and by studying its various expressions and postures, artists can convey a wide range of emotions and narratives in their artwork. Whether it is the vulnerability of a slouched posture or the strength exuded by a confident stance, the human form offers a rich visual language that artists can utilize to communicate their ideas and connect with their audience on a deeper level.

Furthermore, exploring the human form can also serve as a means of self-expression and self-discovery for artists. By studying and representing the human body, artists can explore their own identities, beliefs, and experiences. Through the process of creating art, artists can uncover hidden aspects of themselves and gain a deeper understanding of their own emotions and thoughts. This introspective journey not only enriches their artistic practice but also contributes to personal growth and self-awareness.

In addition to personal growth, exploring the human form can also contribute to the broader artistic community. By pushing the boundaries of representation and challenging societal norms, artists can inspire and provoke conversations about body image, diversity, and inclusivity. Through their artwork, artists can challenge stereotypes and celebrate the beauty of all body types, fostering a more inclusive and accepting society.

Lastly, exploring the human form allows artists to continuously evolve and refine their artistic skills. The human body presents a myriad of challenges, from capturing the subtle nuances of facial expressions to mastering the proportions of different body types.

Disclaimer

While all attempts have been made to verify the information provided in this book, the author does assume any responsibility for errors, omissions, or contrary interpretations of the subject matter contained within. The information provided in this book is for educational and entertainment purposes only. The reader is responsible for his or her own actions and the author does not accept any responsibilities for any liabilities or damages, real or perceived, resulting from the use of this information.

The trademarks that are used are without any consent, and the publication of the trademark is without permission or backing by the trademark owner. All trademarks and brands within this book are for clarifying purposes only and are the owned by the owners themselves, not affiliated with this document.

You want to learn how to draw the human figure

The problem is you don't know where to start. You've looked at books in craft and books stores and have even gone online, but there are still questions and techniques that puzzle you. You've tried following the tutorials, but questions arise, and you have found steps missing in the process. You flipped back in the book to see if you missed anything and found the missing step wasn't something you've overlooked.

This book is a comprehensive guide. I will walk you through basic techniques before starting the lessons. You will be walked through steps not found in other books to help you get a better grasp on how to draw the human figure, and it's all done in an easy-to-follow format. So, what are you waiting for?

You're on your way to drawing the human form.

The most complex subject to draw is the human form. No human is the same in detail, but, at its base, it is the same. Proportions and height are the same and can be drawn with simple techniques which haven't been in other books you've read and tried to follow. This book is designed to teach you:

- The basics of shading

- The form of the head and how the features are arranged on it,

- The basic proportions of the body,

- How to add details to the human form

- How to draw the form in motion,

- How to draw expressions on the face

If all this seems a lot to take in, don't worry. Each chapter covers the different techniques. I will walk you through each of the methods and not leave you scratching your head. If you're ready to start learning, read on, my friend, and let's get started.

Chapter 1 – Tools of the trade

A doctor needs medical tools; a carpenter needs wood working tools, and you also need the right tools to break into your new hobby. Below is a list of the basic you will need to get started.

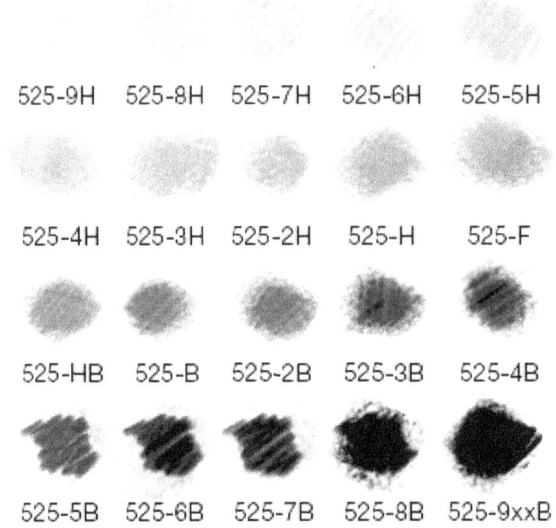

Pencils

In the art world, there are sketching and drawing pencils that are graded by the hardness of the lead. These grades all have a purpose from lightly laying out the piece to shading the figure to add in the finishing touches.

All of these grades mark the paper differently. Below is a basic chart for the different grades of pencil leads.

Pencil Sharpeners

Any basic pencil sharpener will do.

Erasers

There are many erasers on the market you can use to help you draw the human figure:

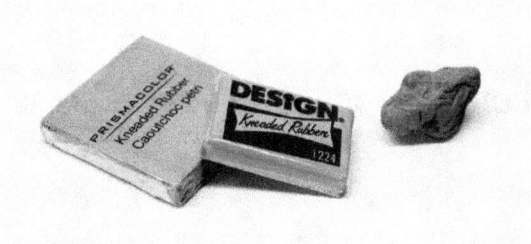

• Pink Eraser: This is the most common eraser and you can find it in any store. This erases any pencil mark on the page.

• The gray kneaded eraser can help with smudging and shading. You can pull it into any shape you want to lighten pencil marks and help with shading.

Eraser guard

To your left is a tool that can help you get rid of stray pencil marks without touching the lines you wish to keep.

Dry Erase

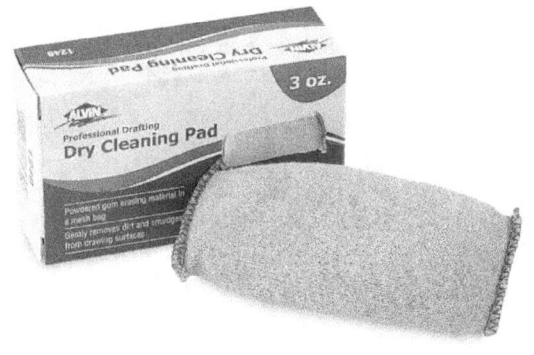

This can come in handy with stray marks as you work and accidental smudges caused by your hands going across your artwork. Shake it on your paper and rub it in the places you want to clean up.

Paper

There a sketch pads in different sizes you can use to get started.

Your work space

You should be seated at a desk with a surface you can tilt upward. This will allow you to draw comfortably. Your chair should allow you place your feet on the floor without having scoot forward in it, and your chair should be comfortable enough for you to sit in for long periods of time without your legs going to sleep or your back hurting.

Felt or fine tip marker

If you wish to immortalize your work of art, inking pens, felt tip pens, and even an extra fine Sharpie can help. I would suggest starting with the most economical until you get the hang of it.

Blending Stumps

To the left are blending stumps and they are usually sold in packs. They allow you to blend shading easily.

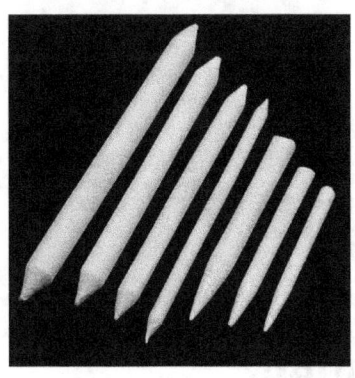

Chapter 2 – Shading and Color Play

Nothing brings a figure to life than shading it just right. Shadows and shading correctly can make the figure come to life and give it depth and character. In this chapter, we will go over the basics of shading and the technical aspects behind them.

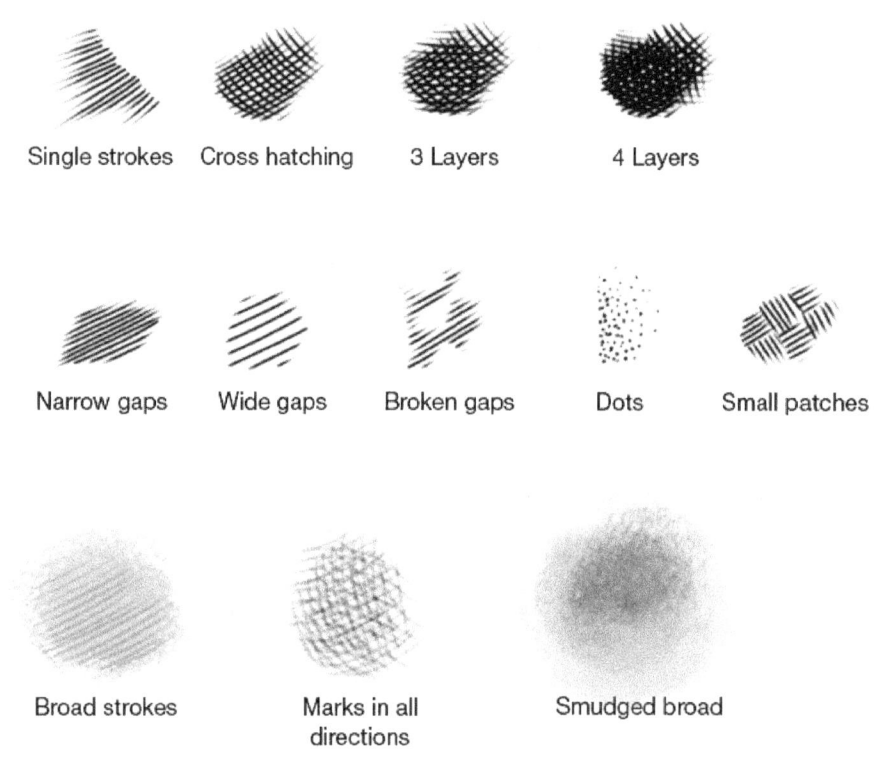

| Single strokes | Cross hatching | 3 Layers | 4 Layers |

| Narrow gaps | Wide gaps | Broken gaps | Dots | Small patches |

| Broad strokes | Marks in all directions | Smudged broad |

Shading techniques

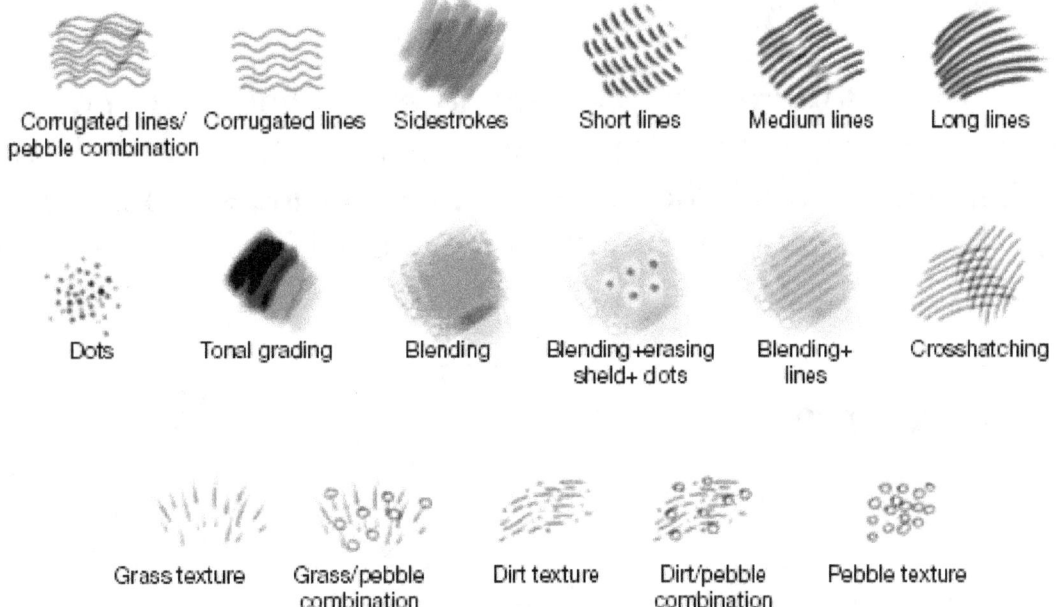

Corrugated lines/ pebble combination   Corrugated lines   Sidestrokes   Short lines   Medium lines   Long lines

Dots   Tonal grading   Blending   Blending+erasing sheld+ dots   Blending+ lines   Crosshatching

Grass texture   Grass/pebble combination   Dirt texture   Dirt/pebble combination   Pebble texture

To the left are the different types of shading techniques you can employ in drawing your subject. Each of these techniques is used in different cases and in different areas of the drawing. The ones you will be using in these lessons will be cross hatching, broad strokes, and smudged broad techniques.

Dots can be used in cases of neck shading and shading between fingers and other digits as well.

Textures in shading

These textures can be used to enrich your drawings and can add details without having to draw them in so they are dark. Grading, for instance, can tell the person who is looking at your piece of art how far the light is away from your subject and at what angle the light is at.

Light source

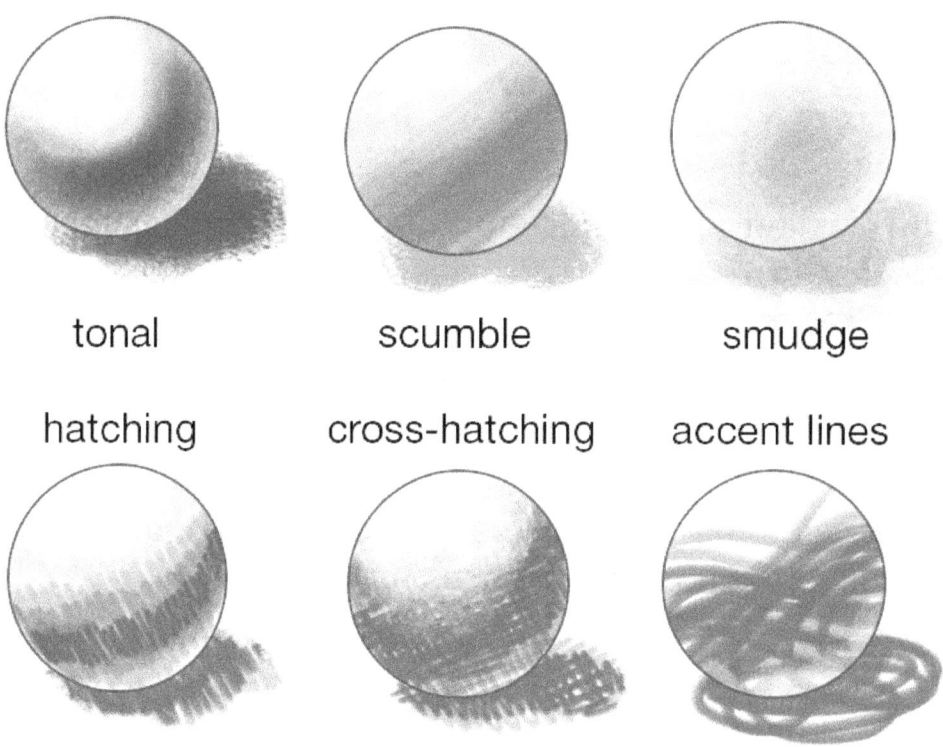

tonal   scumble   smudge

hatching   cross-hatching   accent lines

Here we have incorporated some of the shading techniques to show you how to shade according to where the light source is. The light source is top left, and you can tell from the lightest spot on the sphere. As more and more of the light is blocked by the sphere, the shading gets darker and darker until the light is completely dark at its base.

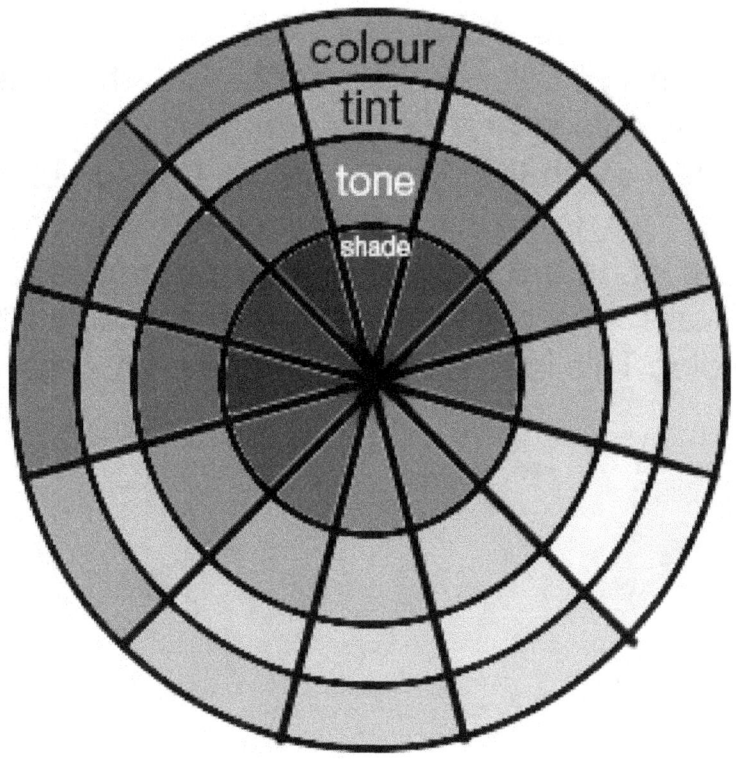

The best way to practice shading is to take simple objects and place them under an adjustable light. Take note of how the shadows grow, shorten, and disappear according how far or close the light happens to be to the object. You can also see how the shadows play on the object itself. This will help you get a better idea of how you shade your subject.

The Color Wheel

We first were introduced to playing with colors when we were young. Crayons and coloring books allowed us to combined colors and even use colors we've never seen to add hues to the pages and characters on them.

What we didn't know was that we were being taught how to use colors.

How to read the wheel

The primary colors are north, south, east, and west. Complimentary colors are to the left and right of these primary colors. They work with the primary colors to add richness and depth. The colors across from the primary colors are contrasting colors. These combinations are used to highlight details and bring attention to certain details. The closer you get to the middle of the wheel, the darker the color. This is to aid in the shading process.

Chapter 3 - The Head and face

The multi-faceted features of the face can be daunting. If you don't get the features right, the face looks off or alien. It isn't pleasing to the eye. Add to this moving the head and adding expressions and you've got a frustrating part of the body to draw and get anatomically correct.

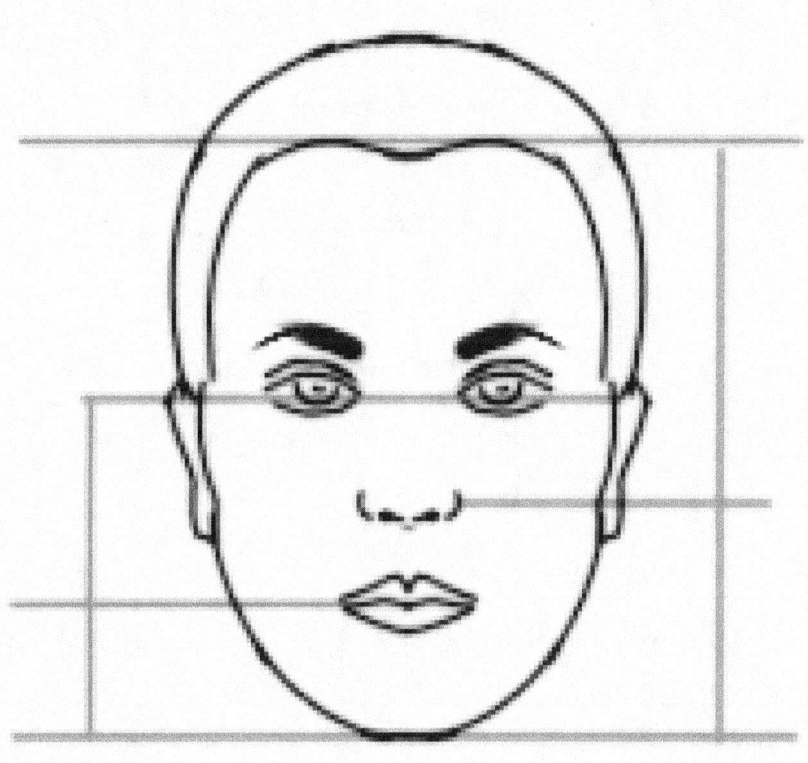

To the left, we see a basic, male head. Think of the start of this head as an oval and draw it on your paper.

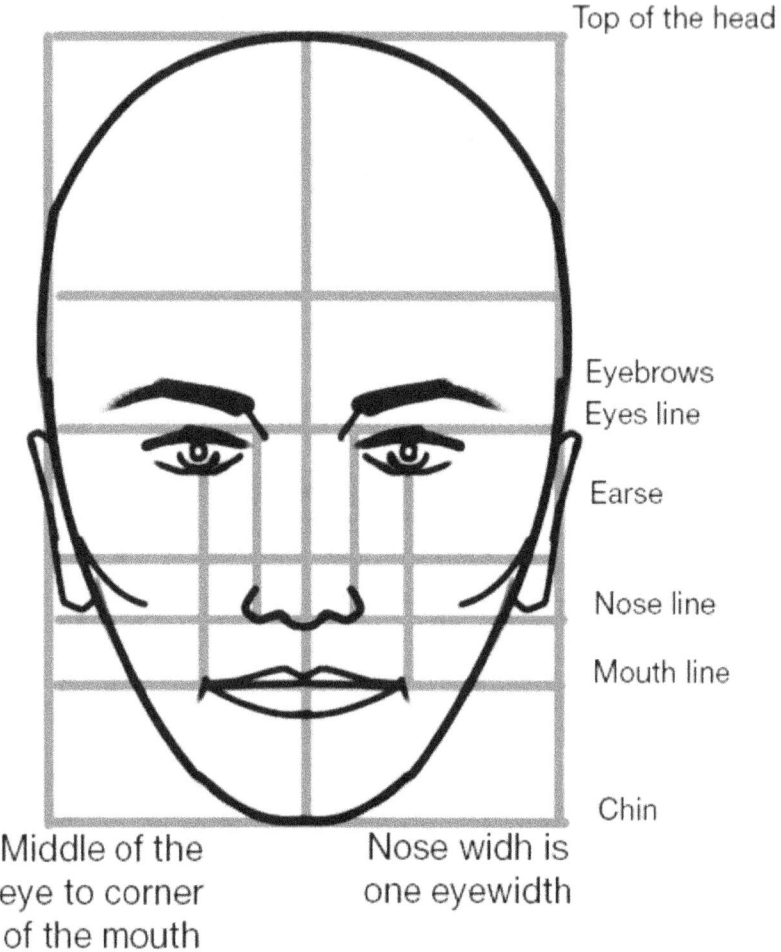

Top of the head

Eyebrows
Eyes line

Earse

Nose line

Mouth line

Chin

Middle of the eye to corner of the mouth

Nose widh is one eyewidth

1. Now, cut this oval in half, and you get where the eyes go. Draw this line.

2. Now, break the bottom half of the head into thirds.

3. One third of the way down draws a line for where the nose would go.

4. Draw another line two-thirds down and place another line where the mouth is going to go.

5. About a quarter of the way down, draw a line for the hairline.

6. Now, draw a circle around the oval for the hair.

7. The ears start from the eye line and stop just below the nose line.

8. Between the eye and nose line, add the cheek bones.

9. Add the curve for the hairline.

10. The eyes are almond shaped and have a line just above them.

11. Add the circle inside the eyes.

12. Add the eyebrows.

13. Add your nose by draw one "C" on both side and the dots for the nostrils and a small "V" for the center of the nose.

14. Draw the mouth.

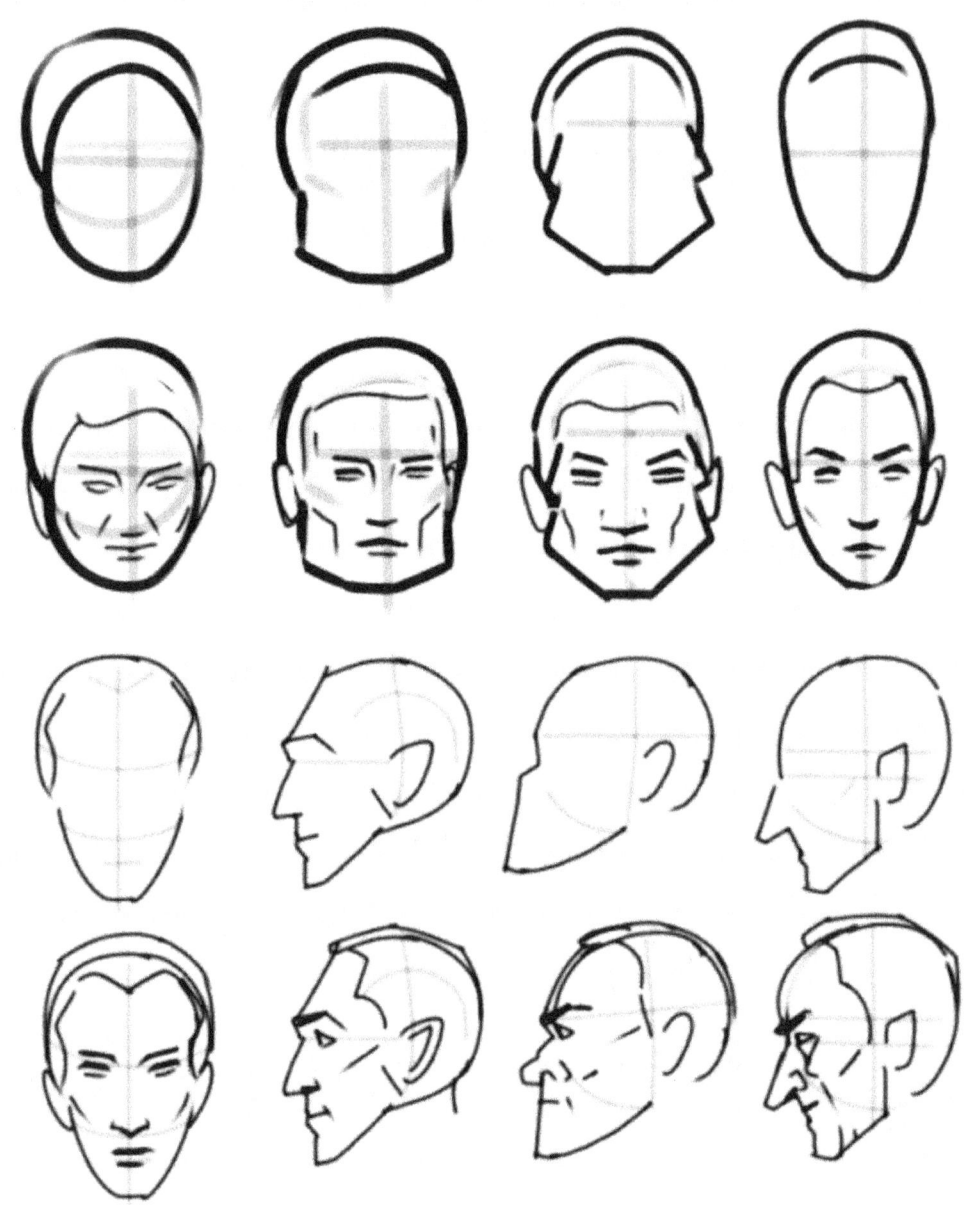

Facial Types

To the left are some of the many types of heads and faces you can draw with practice and laying them out. There are a few things to notice;

1. No matter the shape, they all line up along the "T".

2. Though you use the "T", the face is not symmetrical. The human face isn't symmetrical in real life. Some features are noticeably different.

3. The ear aligns with the eye, no matter the shape of the face.

Tilting the head

When you get into the habit of using the "T" to line up your facial features, you will start to play around with how tilting the "T" will change the direction of the face of the whole. It makes lining up your features easier when tilting the head and making expressions.

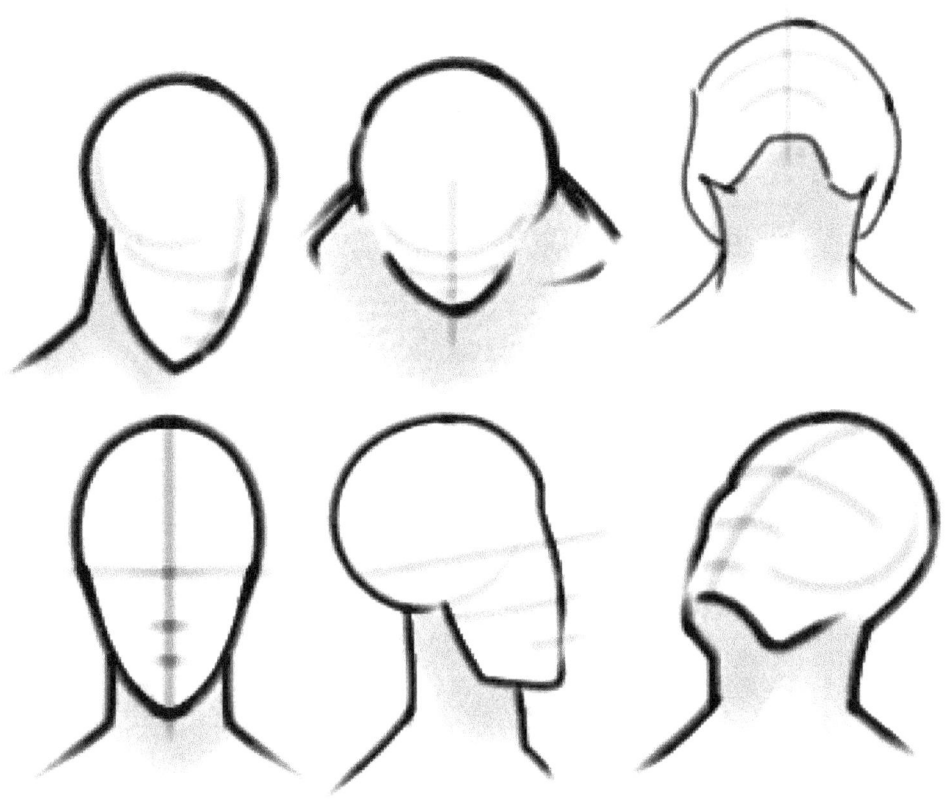

Features and the Profile

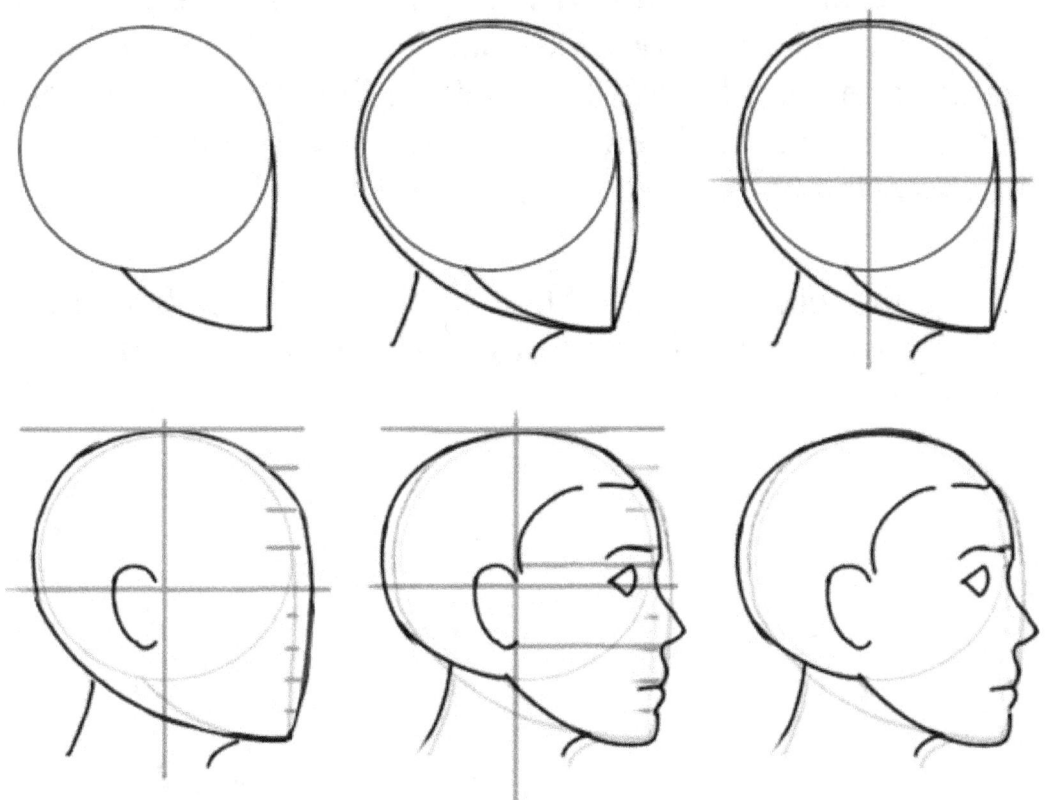

You will inevitably want to draw someone from the side; this is called a profile portrait.

1. Draw a circle.

2. Draw a backwards "L" shape, with the bottom curved.

3. Outline all of it with curves you see in the next step.

4. Add in the two neck lines.

5. The "T" here is different, but it's the same concept as drawing the face from the front. Just add the lines as you see them.

6. Add the features starting with the ear and then the hair line.

Body Proportions

In order to draw a convincing body, you need to be aware of how it is measured and portioned out. the height of the body is measured in head height. The width of the hips is also measured by head height, but the difference is that you would turn the head to the side to get the correct width of the hips.

To the left, is a chart of how to proportion the body according to height? As you can see, an extra head add to the height of the figure as a whole.

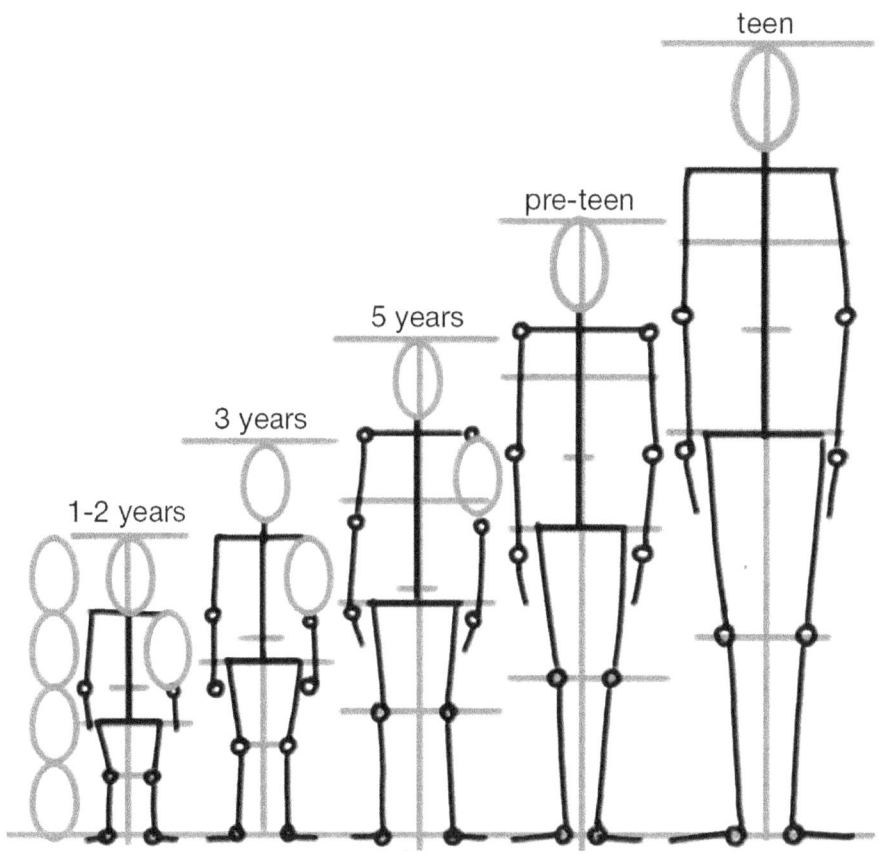

Chapter 4 A study of the human head and face

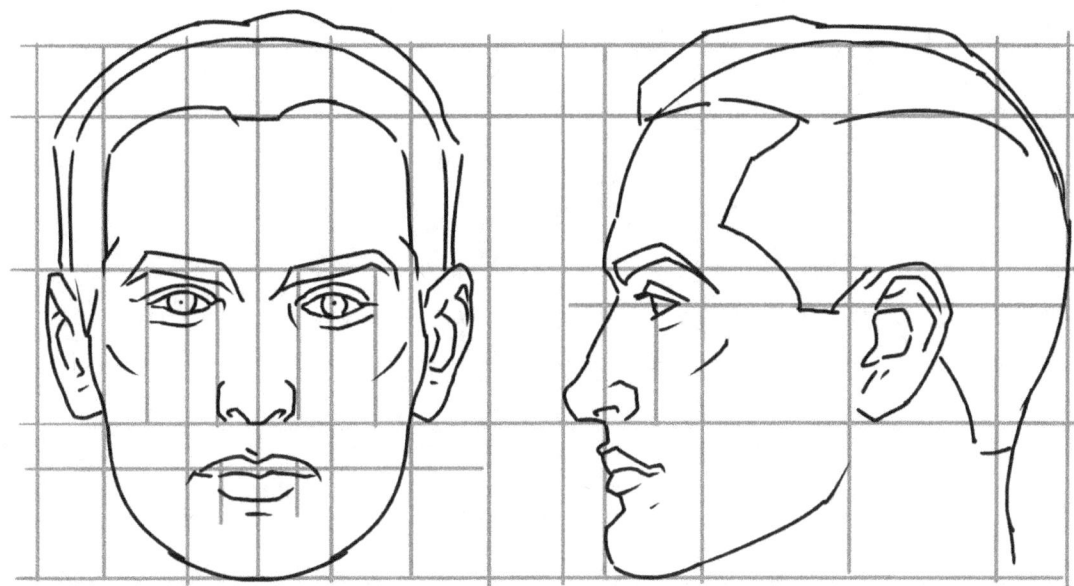

We've covered the basics, and now it's time to delve into drawing the human form in earnest. We're going to start with the head and work our way to the body as a whole.

For the face, we have drawn the template for the face and then added the features.

form layout for future picture

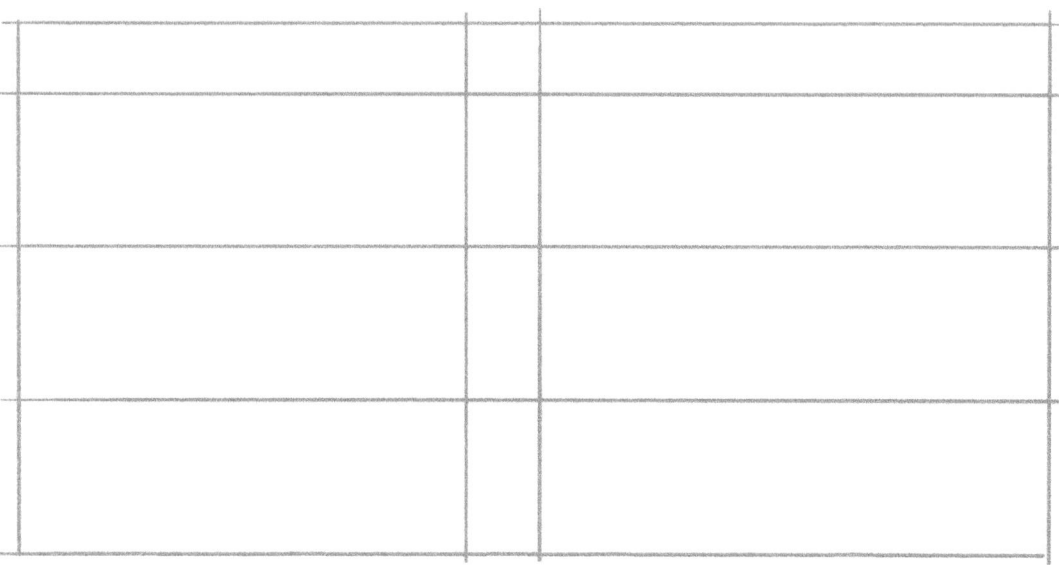

    1. Using the hardest lead possible, draw the layout as you see it to the left.

form more detailed layout for facial features

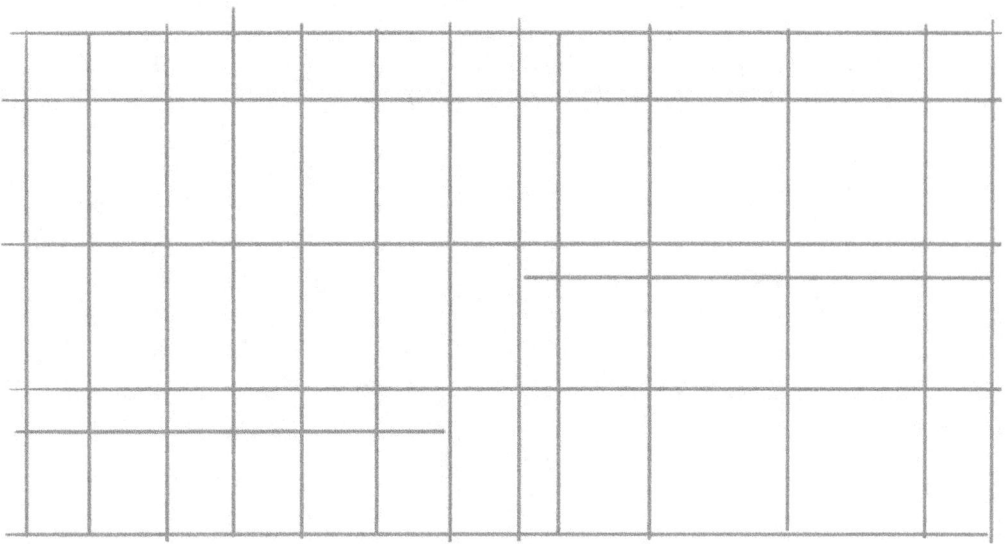

2. Now, add the lines for the facial features.

create the form of brainpan

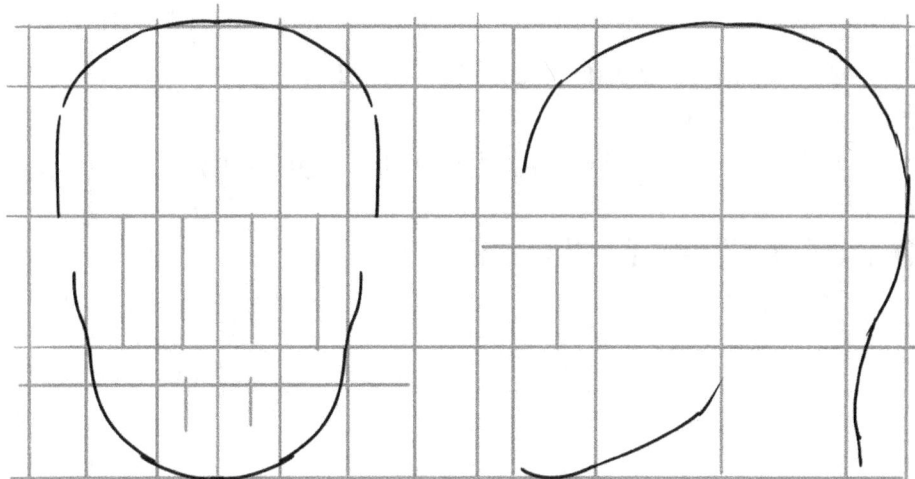

form layout for nose and eyes

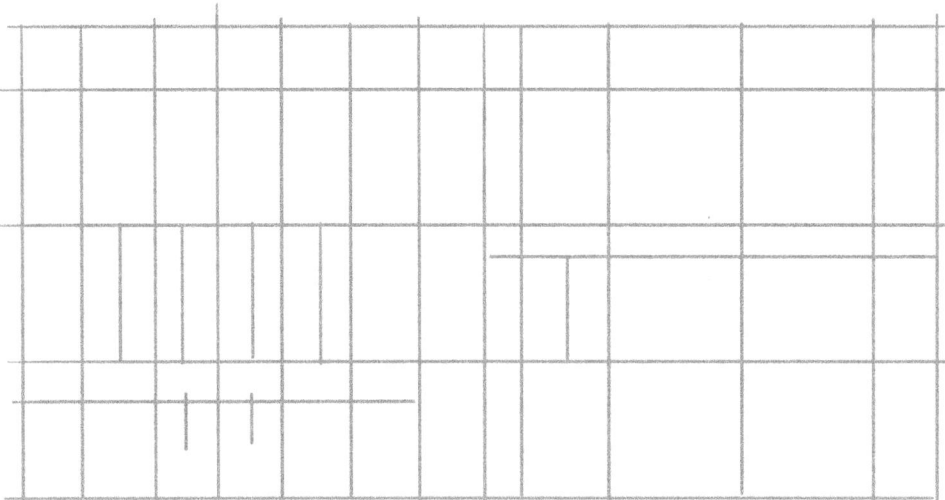

3. Add the guides for the nose and eyes here.

5. Start with the left side of the layout. Add the top of the head.

6. Now, add the lines for the side of the head.

7. Add the bottom of the head.

8. On the right side, draw the curve of the head.

9. Add the lines for the chin.

form facial features and line of eyebrow by layout

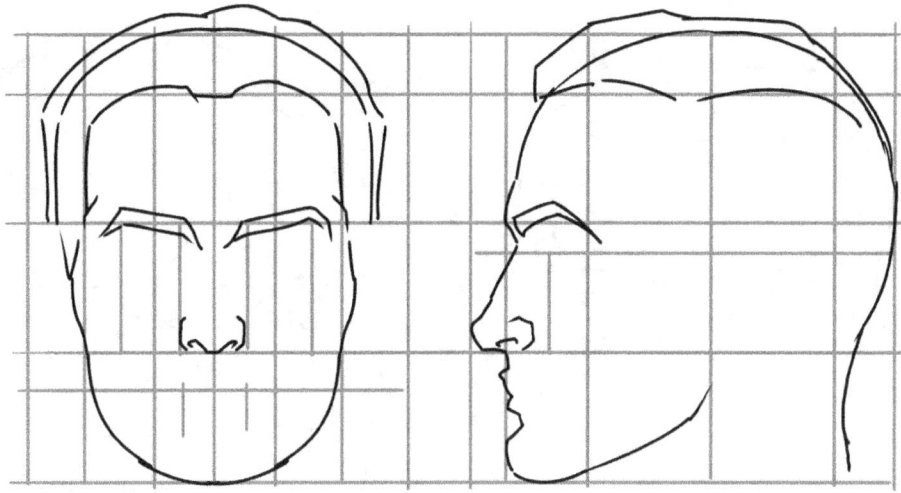

9. On the left of the layout, add the hair line.

10. Add the lines for the hair.

11. Bring the sides of the face up closer to the eye area.

12. Add the eye brows.

13. Add the nose.

14. On the right, add the side of the hair line.

15. Add the curves for the forehead.

draw thr form of eyes,
specify the form f hair

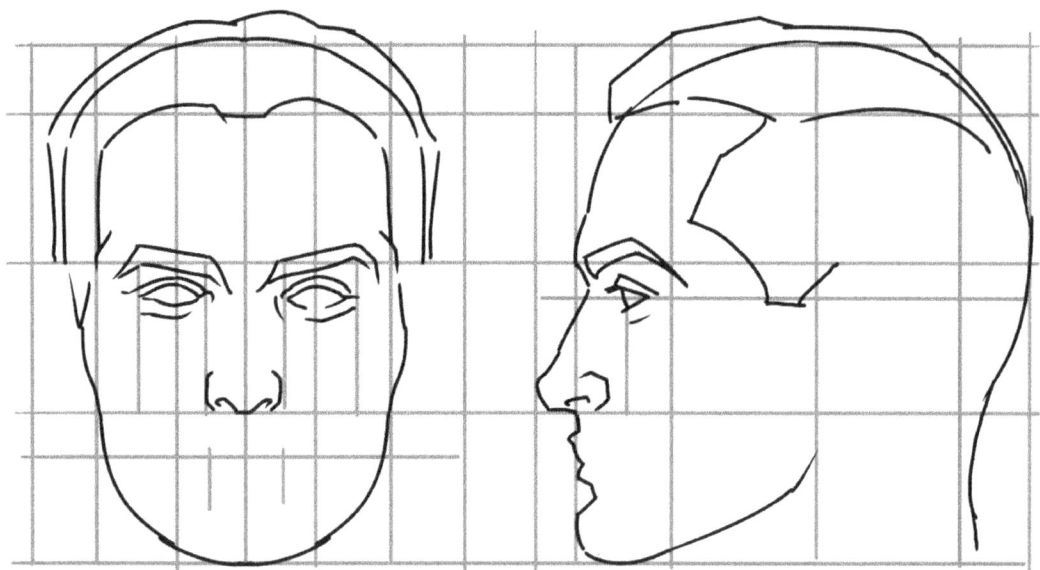

16. Add the nose, keeping inside the guides for the nose.

17. Add the curves for the mouth.

18. Add the chin.

19. Flesh out the hair on both of the sides.

20. Add the eyes according to the guide. Start with the main part of the eye and work outward.

add cheekbone

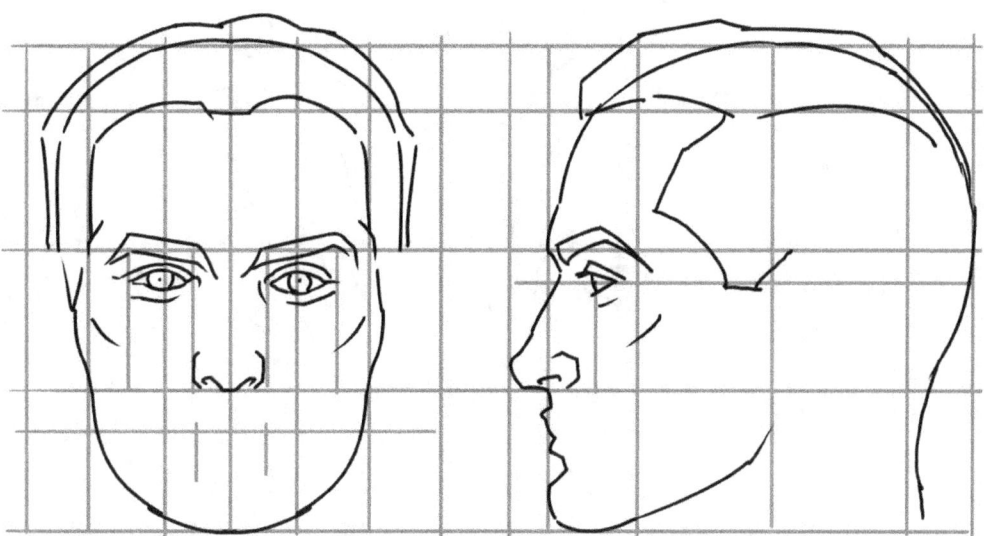

21. Here we add the cheek bones.

22. Add the cornea of the eye.

23. Add the lines under the eye for the bags.

24. You will note on the right half, the eye looks more like a "V". This will make it easier to draw the eyes and add details to them.

25. You can also see where we have put the cheek bones in relation to the profile.

add ear auricle

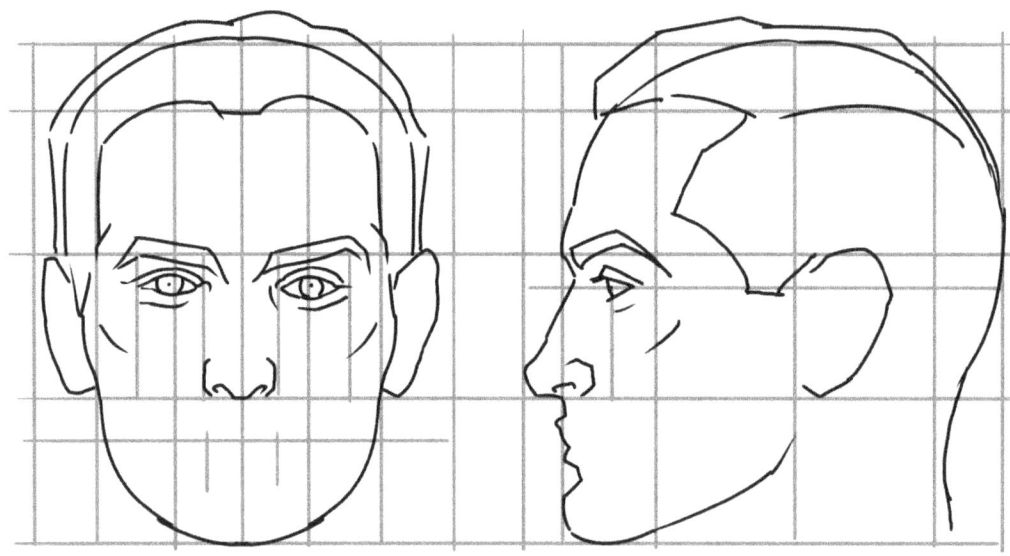

26 On the right, you can see where we have added the ears.

27. On the profile, we've drawn a sweeping curve for the outside of the ear.

28. On the left, we add our first curve starting from the closest to the edge of the ear.

29. We will now add the curve which is the bump inside the ear.

30. Finally, we add the smaller details.

31. On the right, we've worked from the outer part of the ear to the inner part once again.

add lips

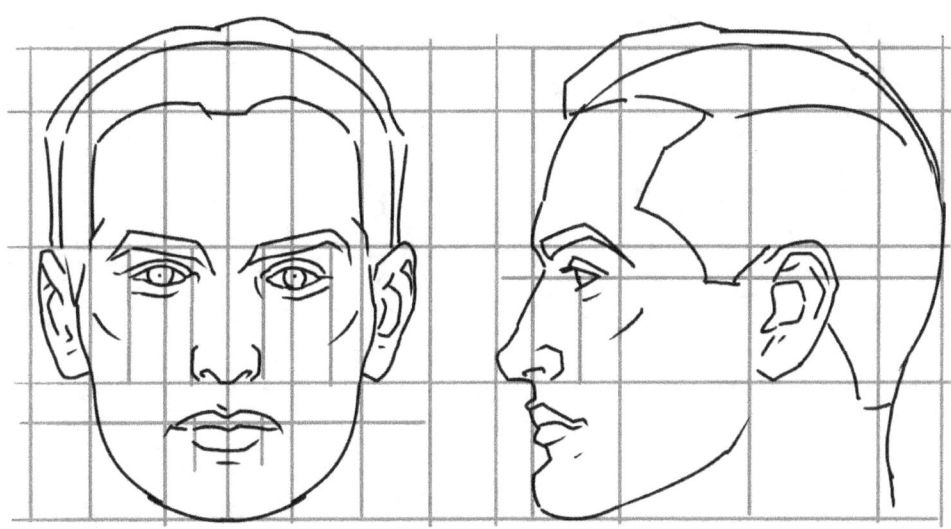

32. The last thing we added was the smaller details.

33. The mouth is added to the left side first with first drawing the curves of the top lip.

34. We then add the line for where the lips come together.

35. Now, add the bottom lip and the line underneath.

36. On the left side, we bring in the lines of the mouth starting from the top lip and working your way down.

form the construction of ear auricle

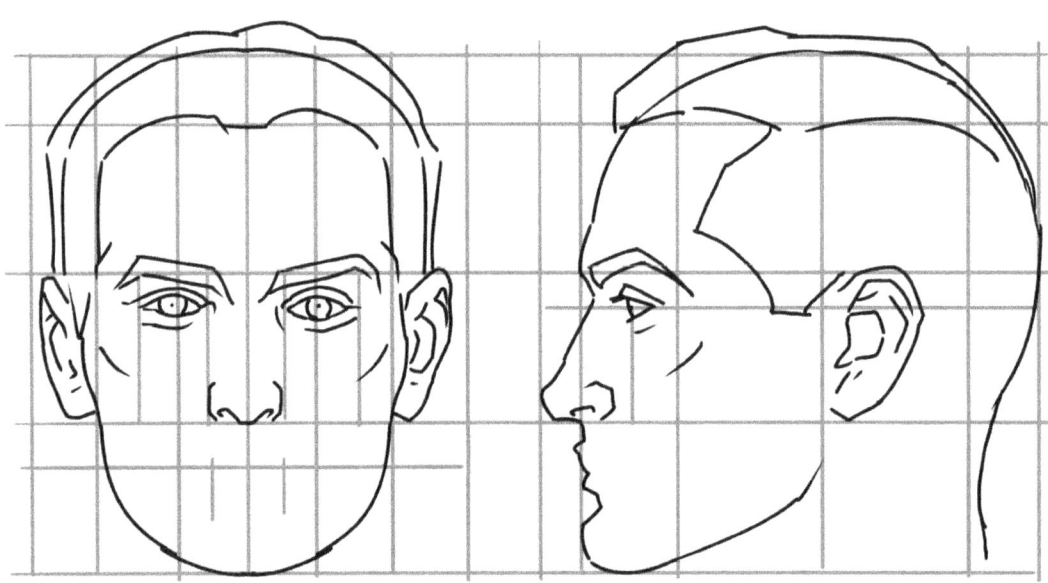

56

Chapter 5 - A Study of the Lips

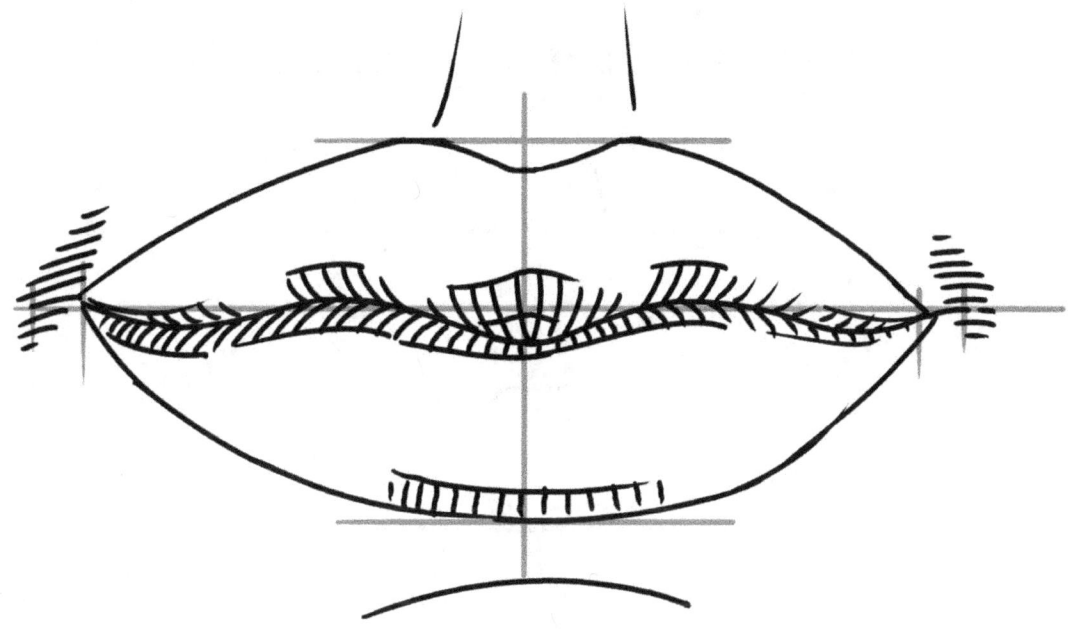

We're taking a closer look at the lips in this chapter and lesson. They look pretty simple to draw, but if you're not careful, it can be the one feature which can ruin a drawing when doing a close-up of the face.

1. This is the basic layout for the lips. You can use this for practice in future pieces.

form layout for lips

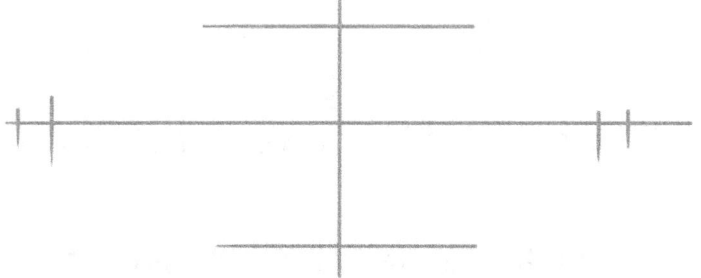

2. We are adding small dashes to help us form the guides for the curves of the lips.

form the contour of upper lip

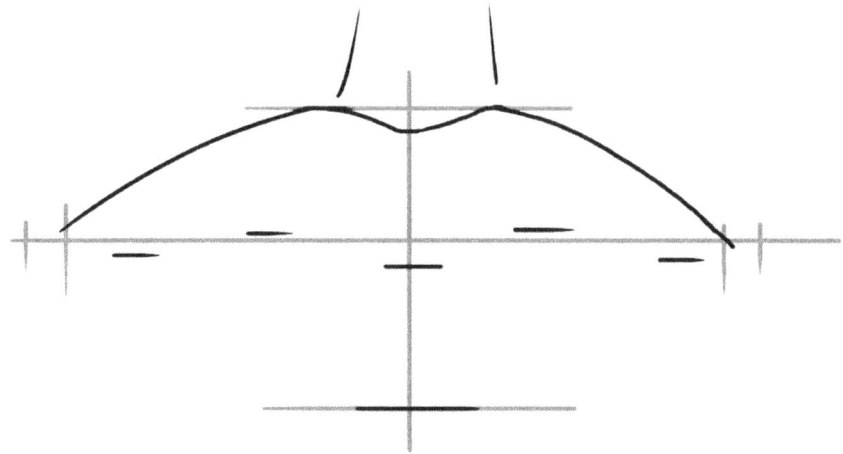

specify the form

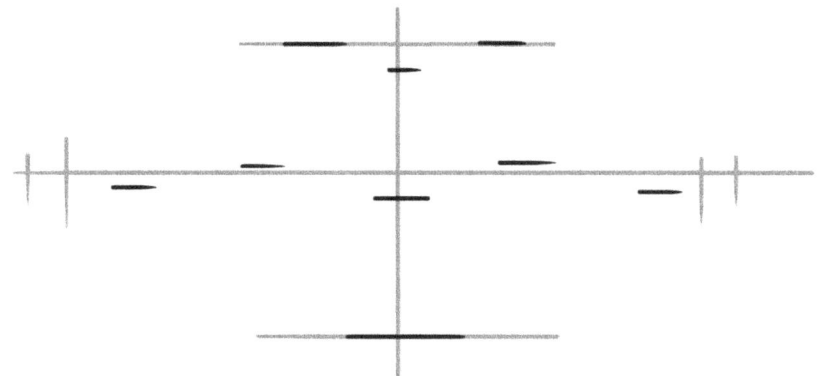

3. Here we see where we put the curve of the contour of the lip.

4. From there, we add the curves on either side of the contour.

4. We add the dashes above the lip for the dip between the nose and mouth.

5. Now, we're using the earlier dashes for the curve between the lips.

draw the contour of lips joint

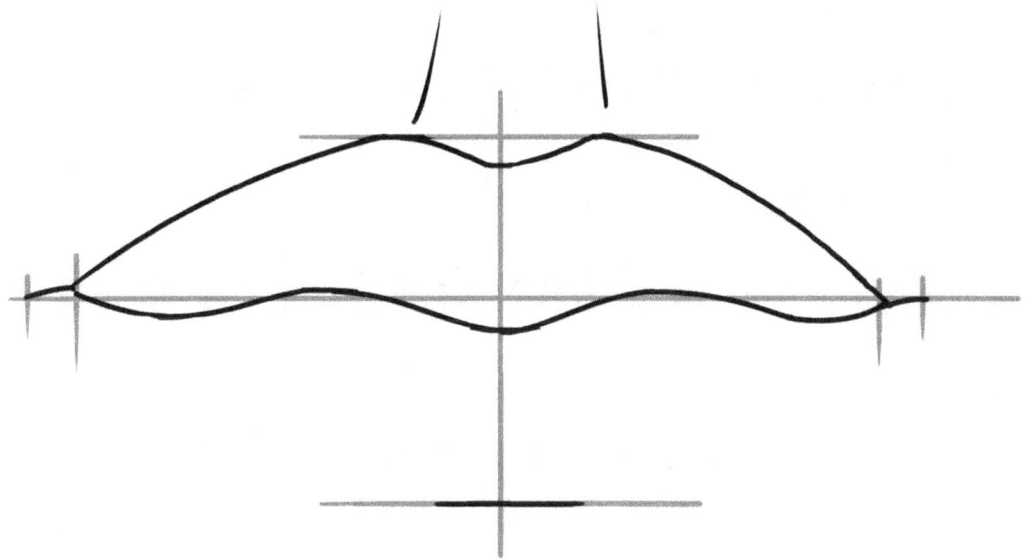

6. Here, we add the bottom curve of the lip.

add the contour of lower lip

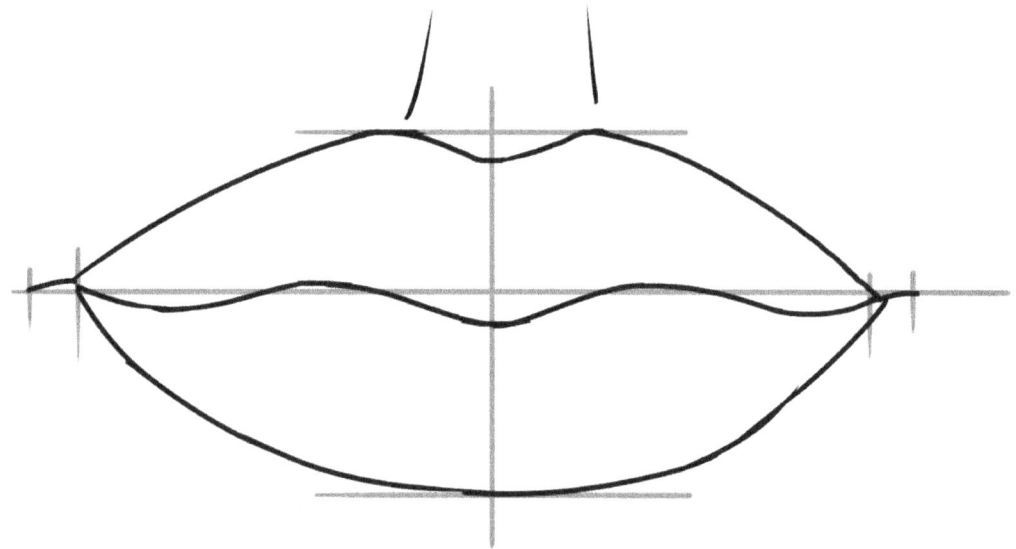

sketch drop shadow

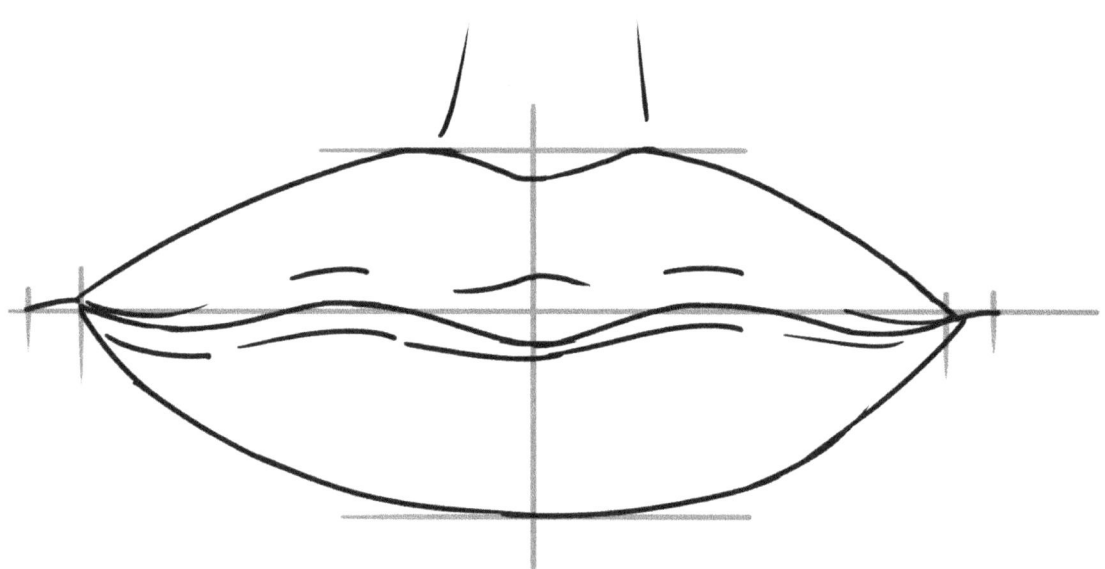

8. Add the extra curves of the lips here.

9. We use hash marks here for shading the lips.

hatch shaded area

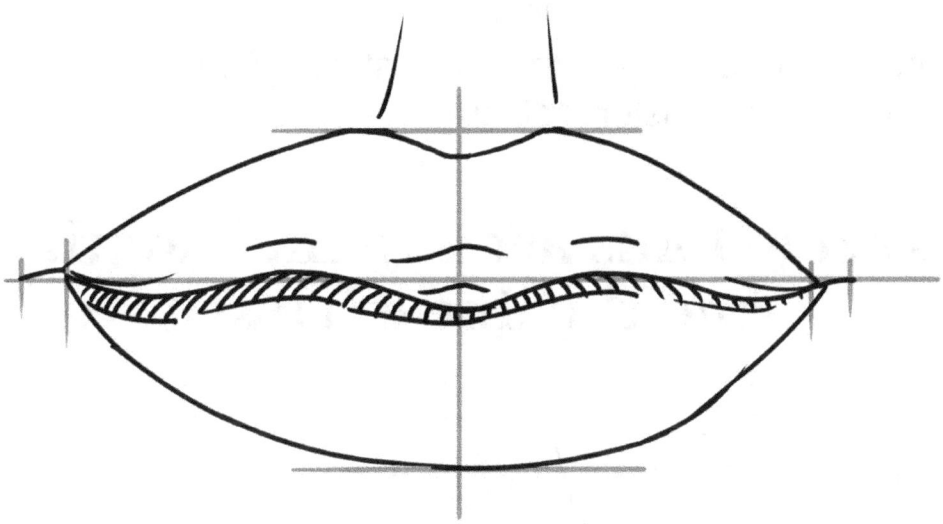

specify the form of lip

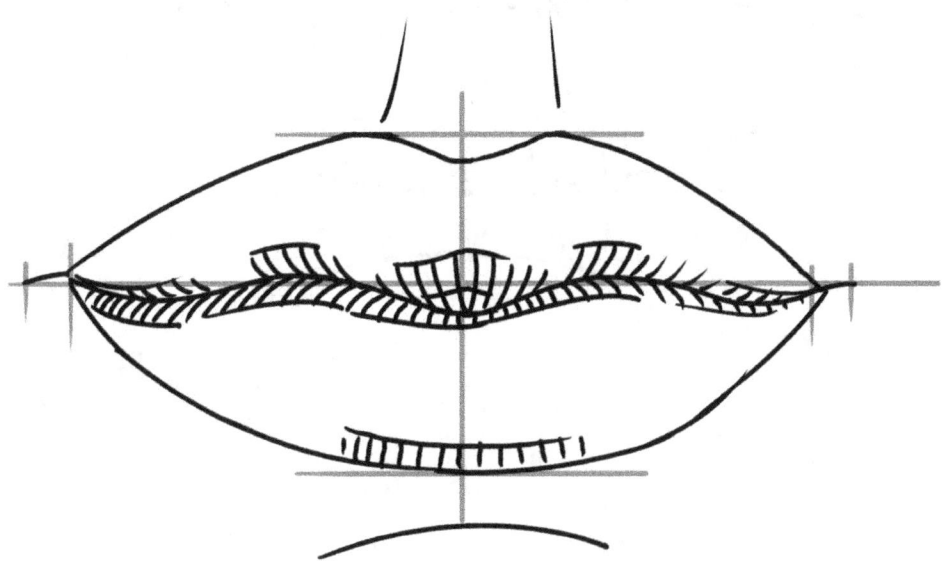

10 We're further specifying the lips by shading them a little more.

11. We have also added the curve under the lip.

Compare what you have done so far and add in the details you don't have on your lesson. You're doing great.

Remember, no one perfect from the start. Even the most notable artists took years to master their craft.

sketch folds around the mouth and the line of chin

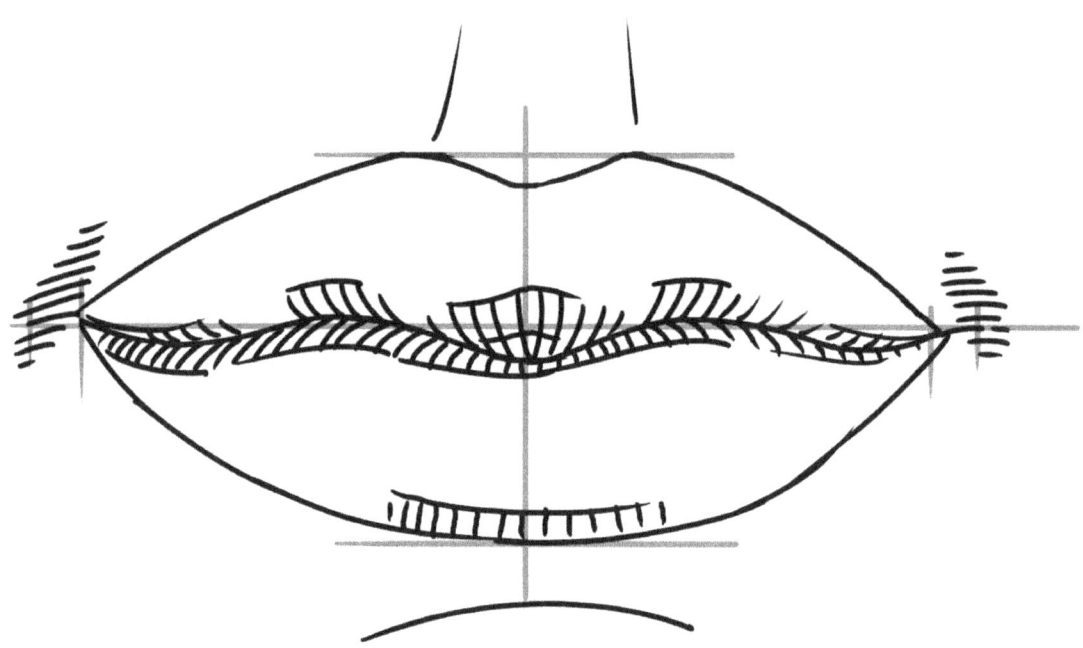

Chapter 6 –A Study of the Nose

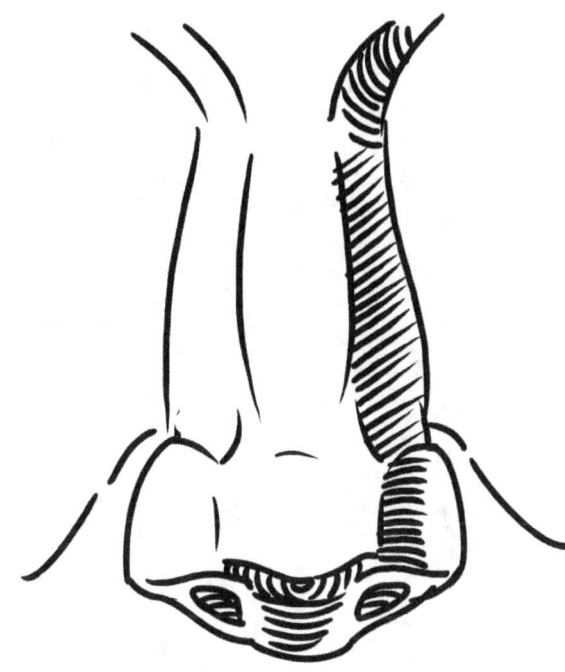

We're going to focus on the nose for this lesson. It can be one of the most daunting features to get right when drawing a face. Though each nose is different and portioned to each individual face, this lesson will help you form the nose a little easier.

form layout for nose

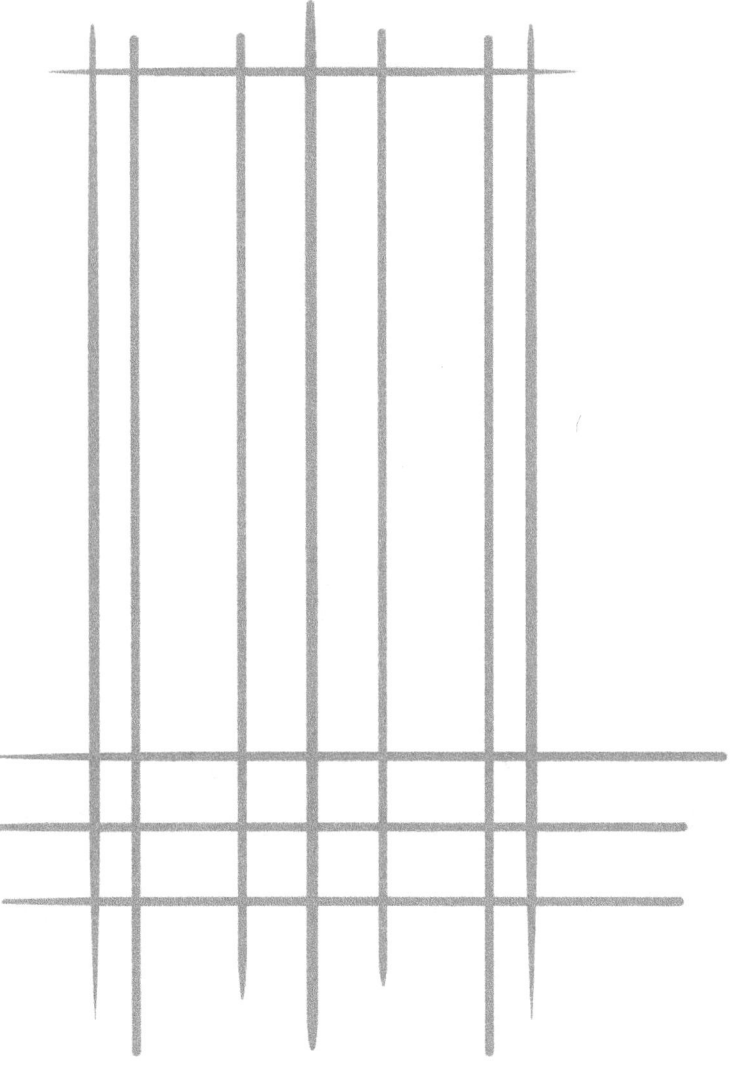

1. This is a basic guide for practicing the nose and all the details.

2. Using the guide, we first add the curves that lead to the eyes.

**sketch nose tip, nose alae
and basis of brow ridge**

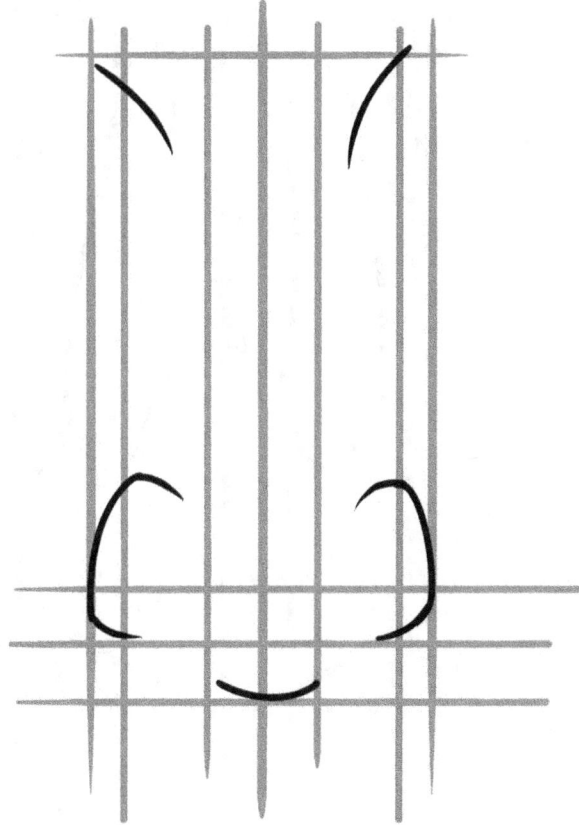

3. We now add two "D"s without the finishing bar for the nostrils.

4. Finally, we add the curve for the point of the nose.

form nasal bone

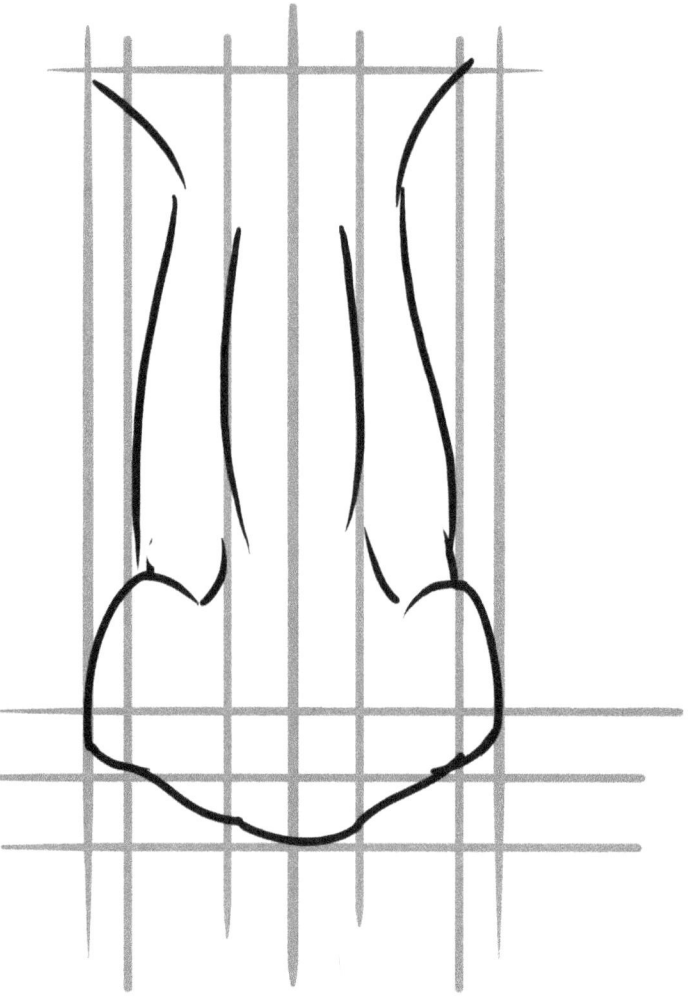

5. We're adding curves to round out the nose.

6. Now, we're adding curves for the top of the nose.

7. Add the curves that will round out the area of the nostrils.

specify the form of brow ridge, sketch the volume of nose

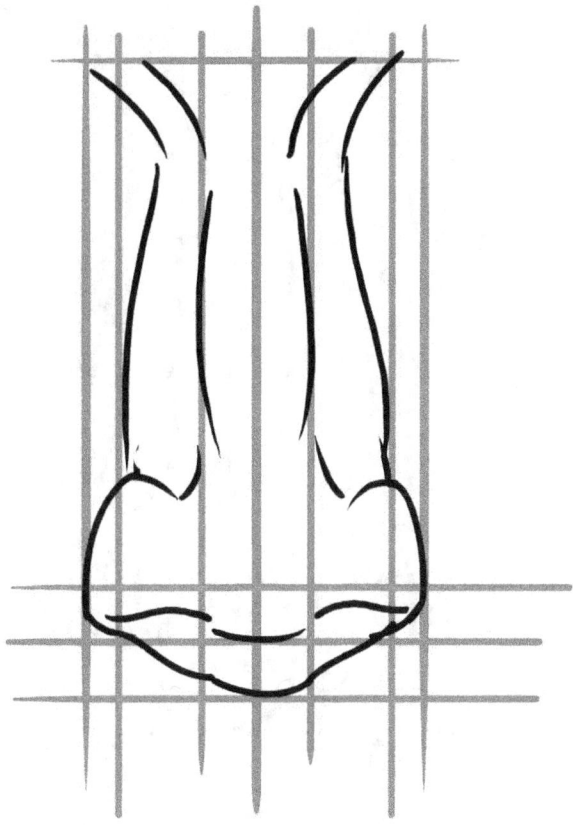

8. Here we're adding outside lines to bulk out the nose a little more.

9. We also added the curves to delineate the nostrils.

add nostrils

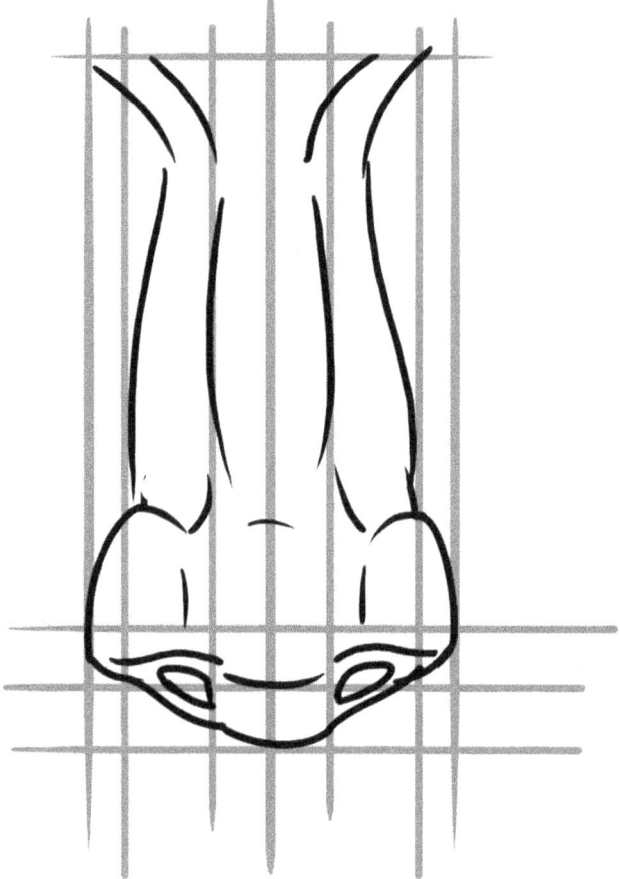

10. We highlight the nostrils a little more here. We start with the awkward circles.

11. We add dashes to further make the nostrils pop out.

12. Add the curves you see coming from the nostril area.

13. Add the shading you see in the picture.

add the shadow at the shaded pieces

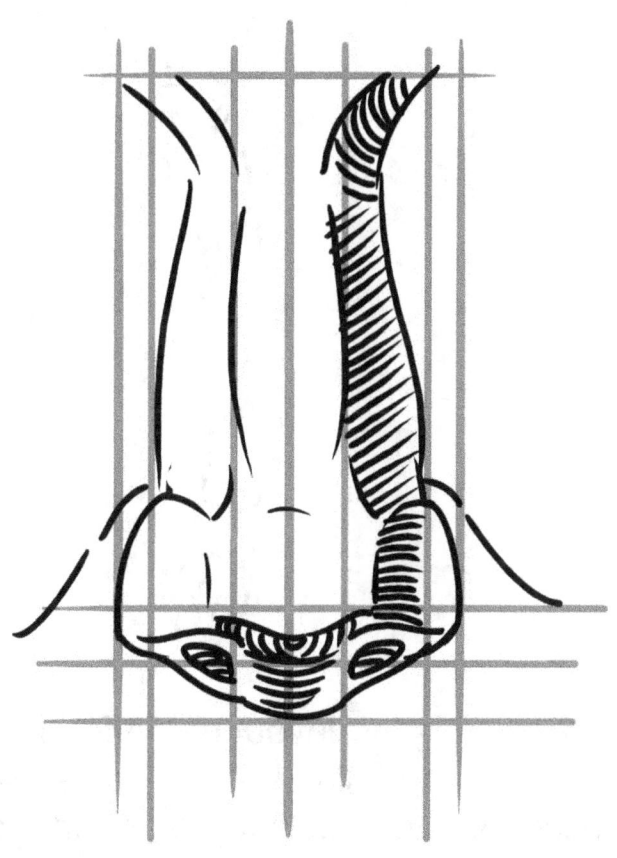

Chapter 7 – The Study of the Arm

Instead of looking at the arm as a whole, look at it as a series on interlocking curves and dashes. When we look at features and equate them with everyday shapes, it makes it easier to draw.

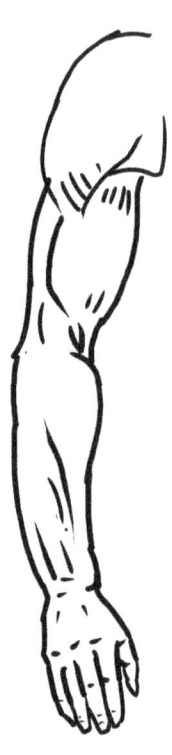

To the bottom left is the layout guide for the arm. This is one of the more simple layouts of the body. Before we use the template below, take notice of the musculature of the arm and how it is defined in the final drawing. Paying attention to these small details is what can make a piece look as if it is ready to pop off of the canvas.

form layout for arm

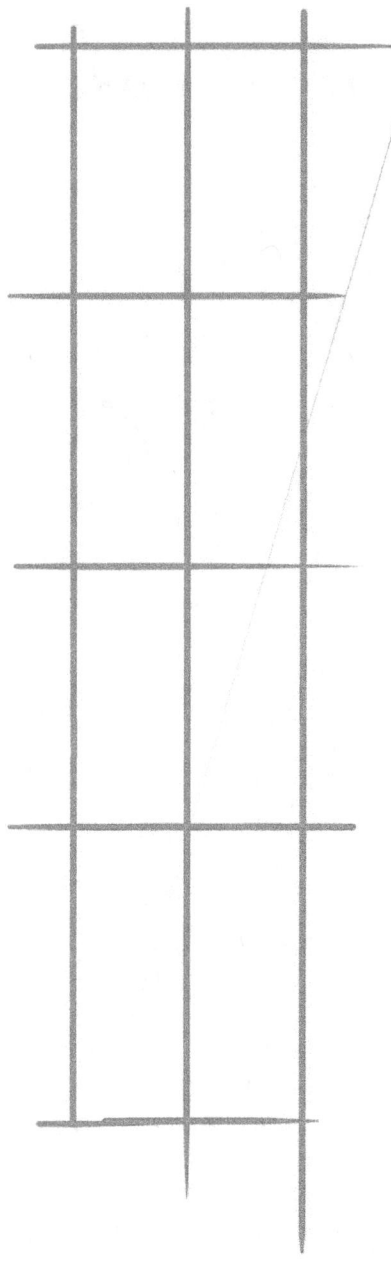

1. We start with the outer curve of the shoulder.

form shoulder joint

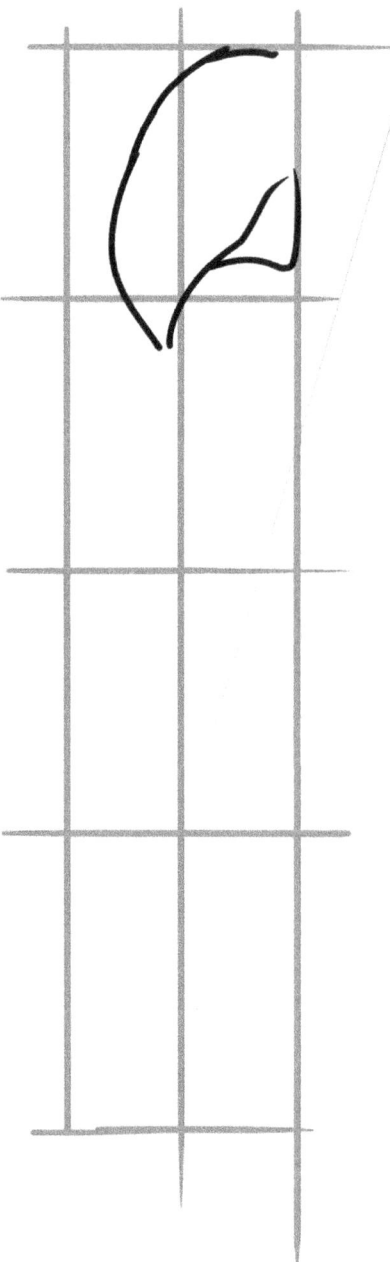

2. We now bring the curve up.

3. Add the final line in between.

add shoulder, specify biceps

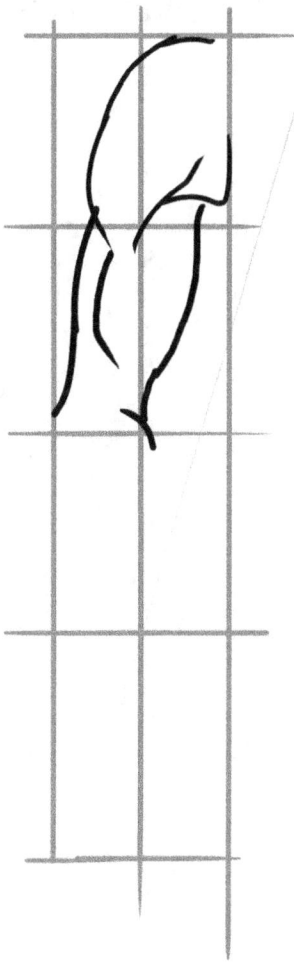

4. Draw the outer curve of the arm.

5. Draw the inner curve of the arm.

6. Draw the line for the muscle.

7. Add the small curve for the elbow.

8. In the crook of the elbow, draw a curvy "V" to highlight the elbow.

add brachia

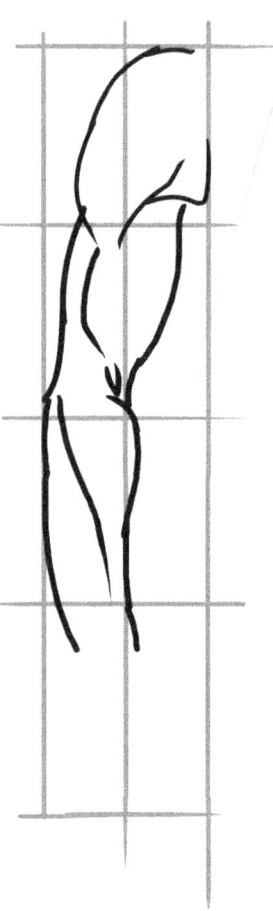

9. Add the curve on the inside of the arm.

10. Add the outside curve of the arm.

11. Add the line delineating the muscle on the forearm.

add hand

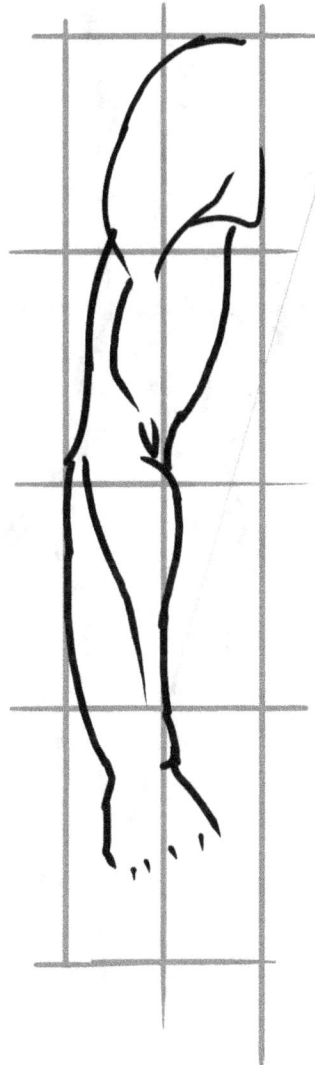

12. Add the curve of the wrist on both sides.

13. Draw the outside of my arms.

14. Add the hash marks for the fingers.

15. Add the lines coming from the wrist and going up the arm.

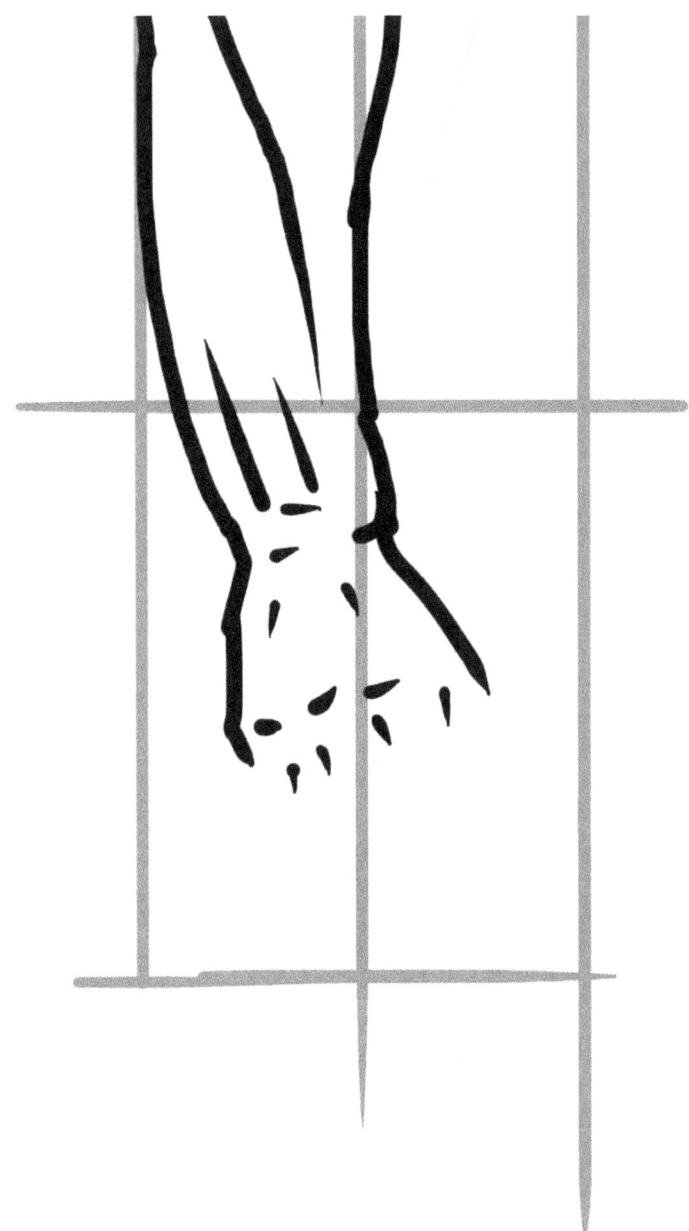

16. Add the dashed dots it the wrist area.

17. Add the accents for the knuckles.

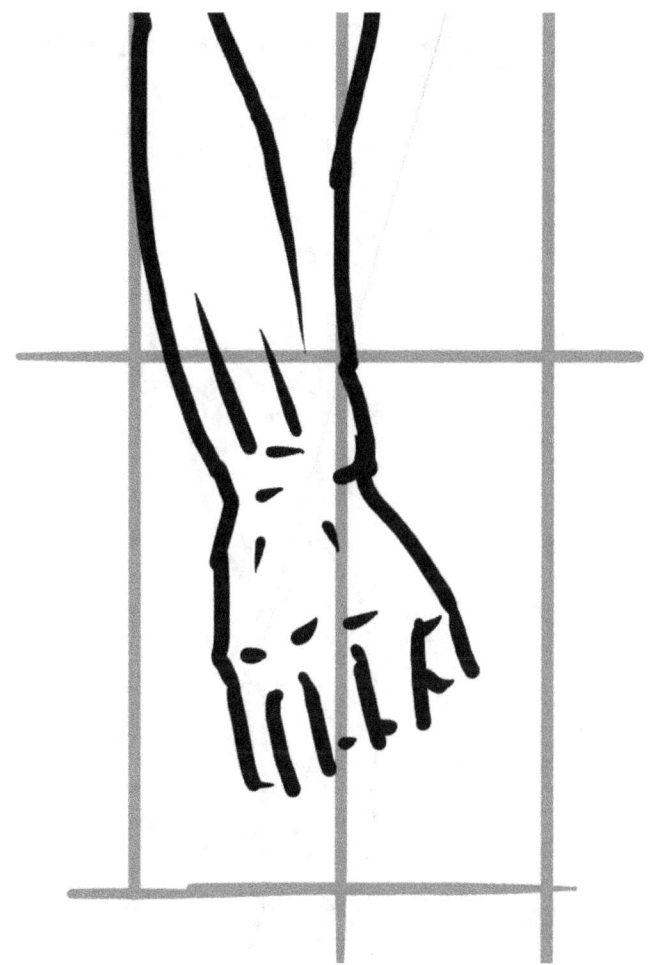

18. Draw in the small lines for the fingers.

19. Here we've finished the fingers.

20. We add dots for the knuckles.

specify arm's muscle

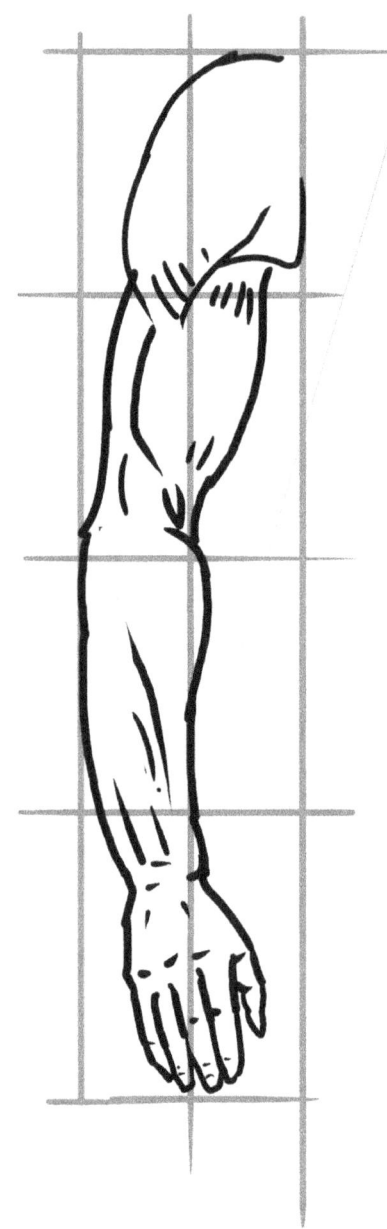

21. Finish the arms by adding the dashes to further detail the muscles of the arm.

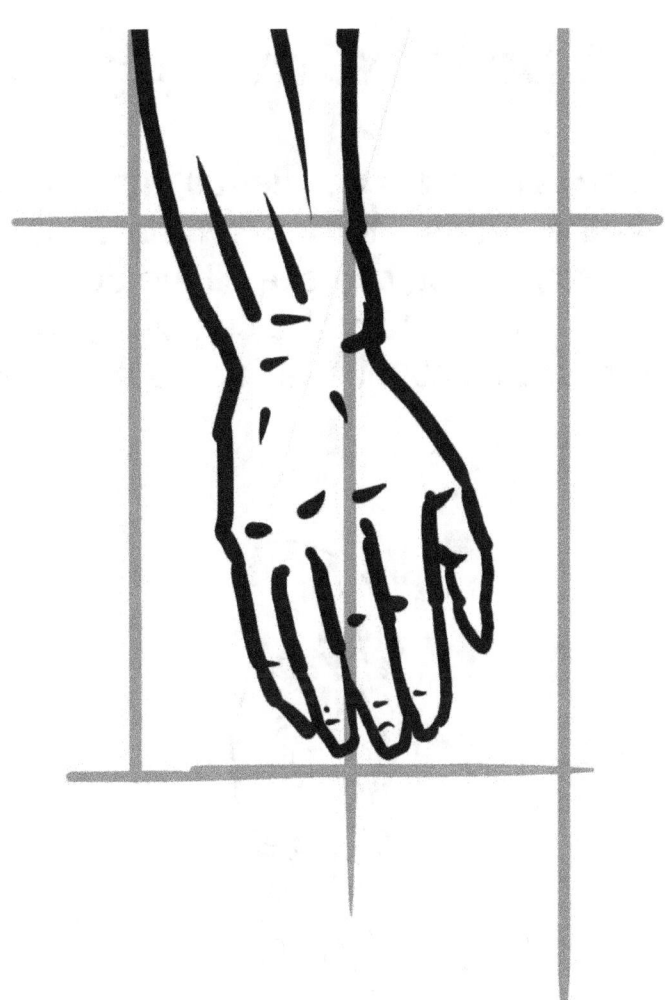

Chapter 8 - A Study of the Leg

The leg can be complex. It is, after all, the part of the body that supports all the other parts, from a physical standpoint. In the sample of the finished leg, you can see all the details of the muscles and how they tie into one another. You can see how the thigh tapers to fit the knee and how the calf muscles flair out.

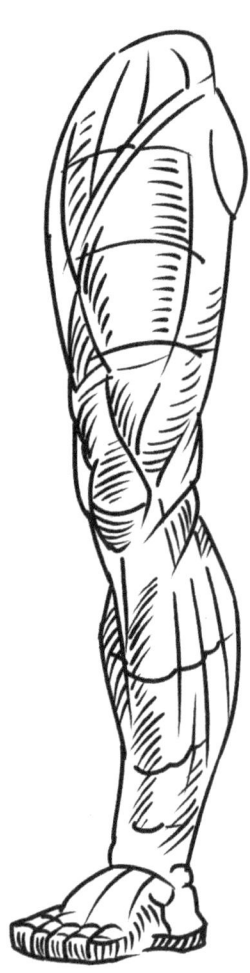

form the layout for leg

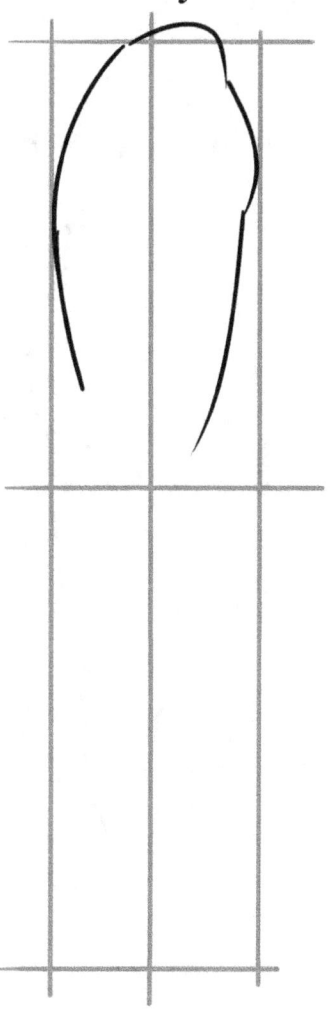

1. Draw the red guide first.

2. Starting from the top, draw your curve down and to the left.

3. Now, draw a slight bump on the right, and a slight curved line.

4. From the right, add a wide angle "L" shape and bring it to the center line of the guide.

form knee joint

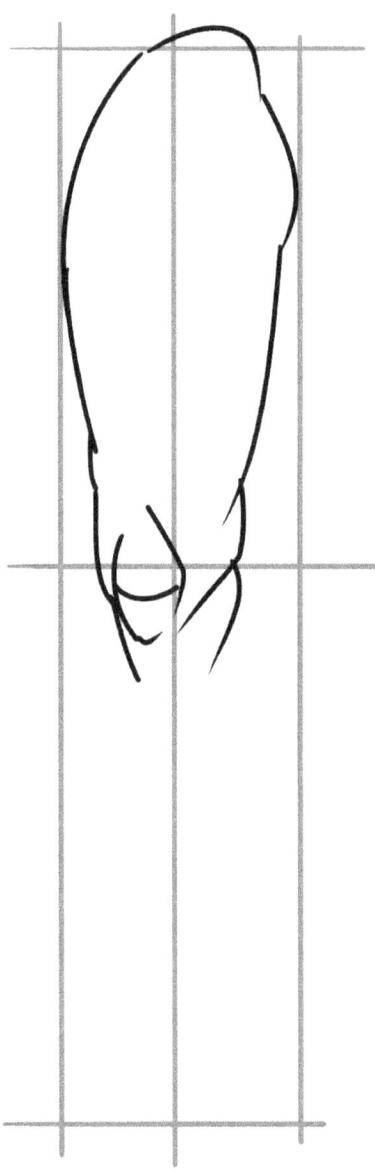

5. Now, draw a bump and a slight on the left.

6. Two loosely drawn triangles make up the kneecap.

7. Draw the curves under the knee.

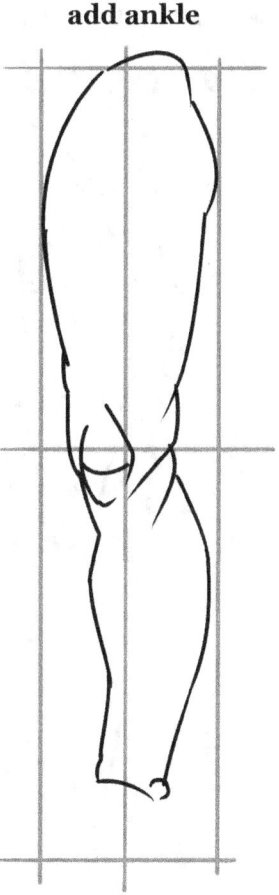

add ankle

8. Draw a wide curve on the right side that tapers in.

9. Draw the bump at the end of the taper.

10. On the left, draw a shorter curve.

11. Add a reverse curve to the first one.

12. Now add the line on the end of the leg.

13. First, draw the "V" shape you seen in the picture.

sketch muscle mass of thigh

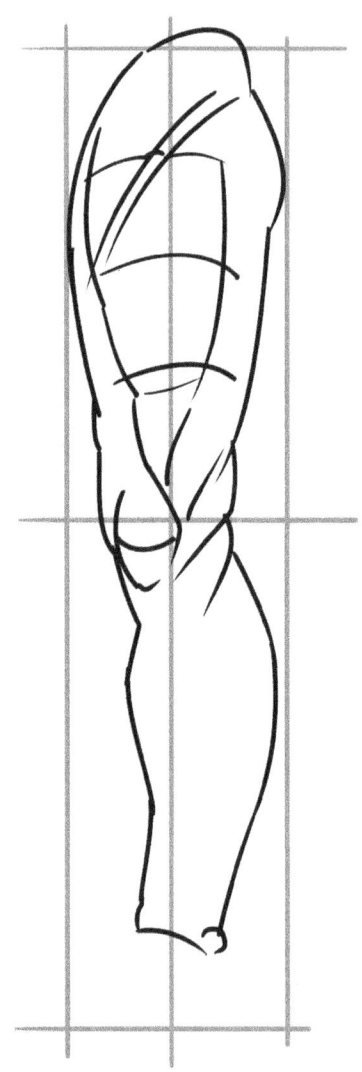

14. Draw the horizontal lines.

15. Finish with the diagonal lines.

16. Bring the line from side of the kneecap to the knee.

Compare your picture so far with what we have here. Add anything you may have left out.

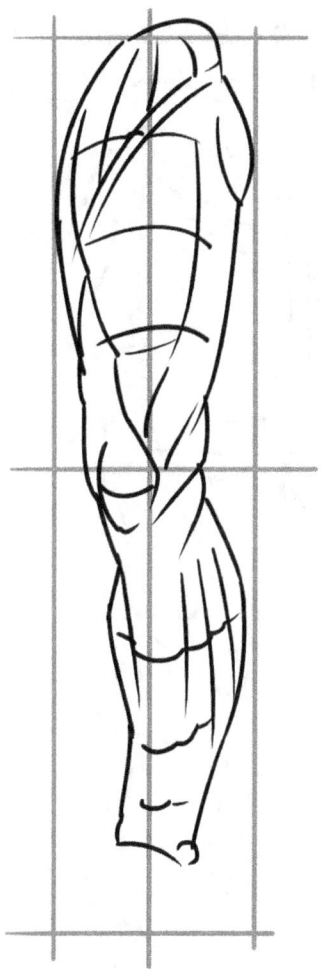

17 Under the knee, add the line vertical lines you see in the picture.

18 Now, add the horizontal ones.

19. Add the two curved lines on the thigh muscles.

20. Then, draw the curve coming up from the bump on the right side of the leg.

21. From the line on the bottom of the leg, draw a hump.

sketch muscle mass of ankle

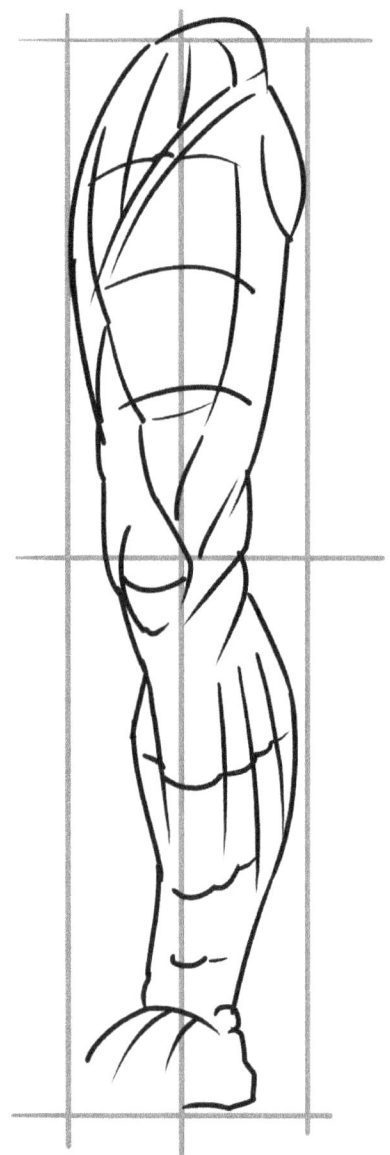

22. Add the lines you see coming from the hump.

form foot

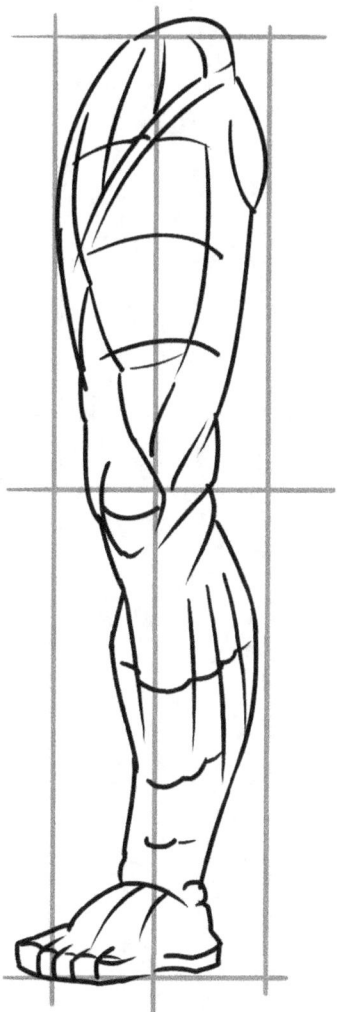

23. Add the back part of the ankle.

24. Draw left-most line coming from the back part of the foot.

25. Draw box shapes for the toes.

26. Draw the lines on the top of the foot to form the toes.

27. Draw the curve for the bottom of the foot.

28. Add any other details you may be missing.

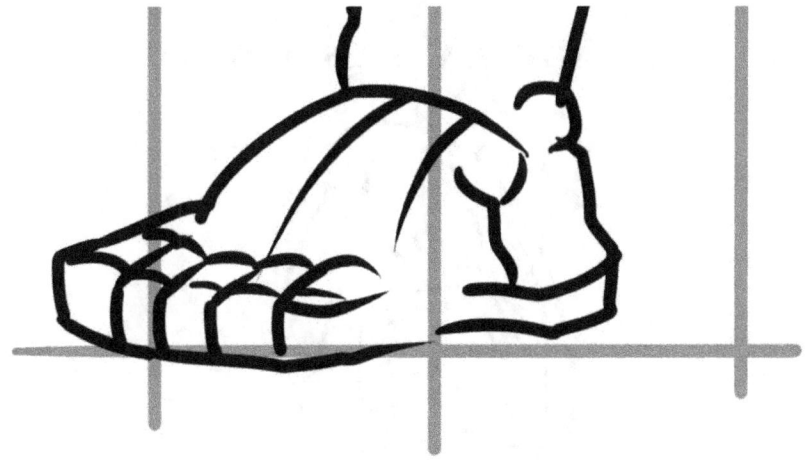

29. Finish out the foot by detailing the toes as you see here.

30. Using hash marks, further define the muscles as you see here.

specify muscles

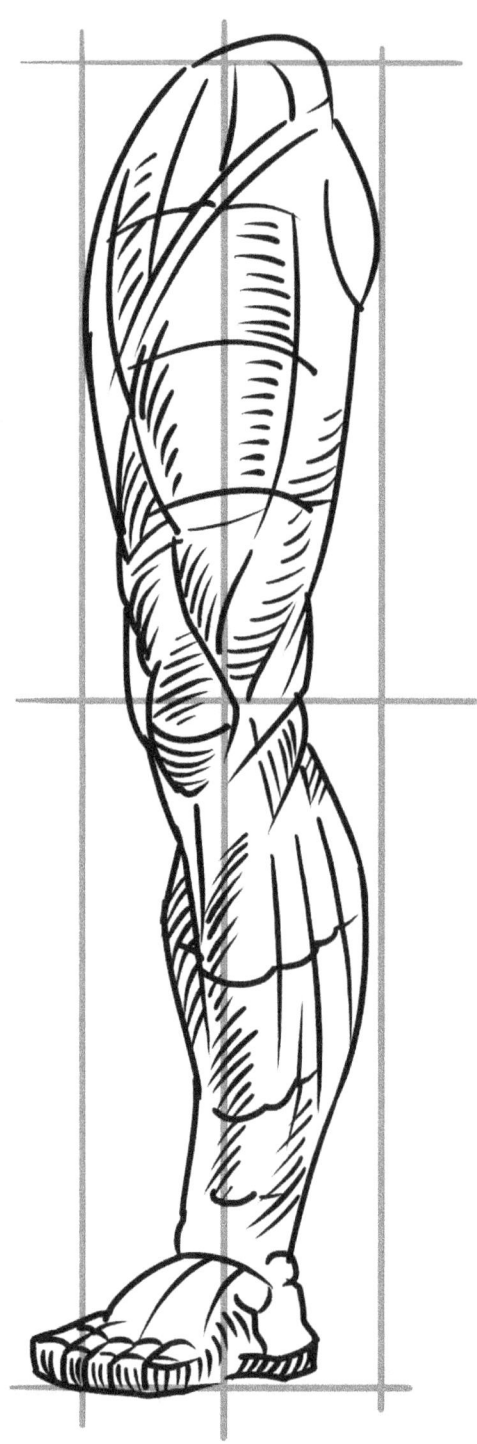

Chapter 9 - A Study of the Female Figure

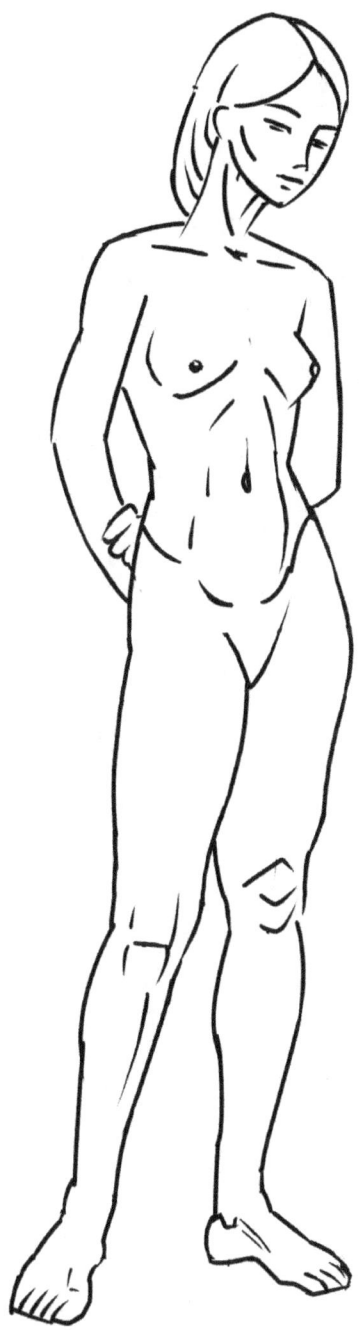

We've studied the basics of shading and formatting. We've delved into drawing the individual parts of the body. Now, that we've done all of that, we are moving into the form in its entirety. We're starting with the female form because it is the more difficult of the two genders to study in art and drawing.

1. Draw the layout on the left.

form layout for female figure

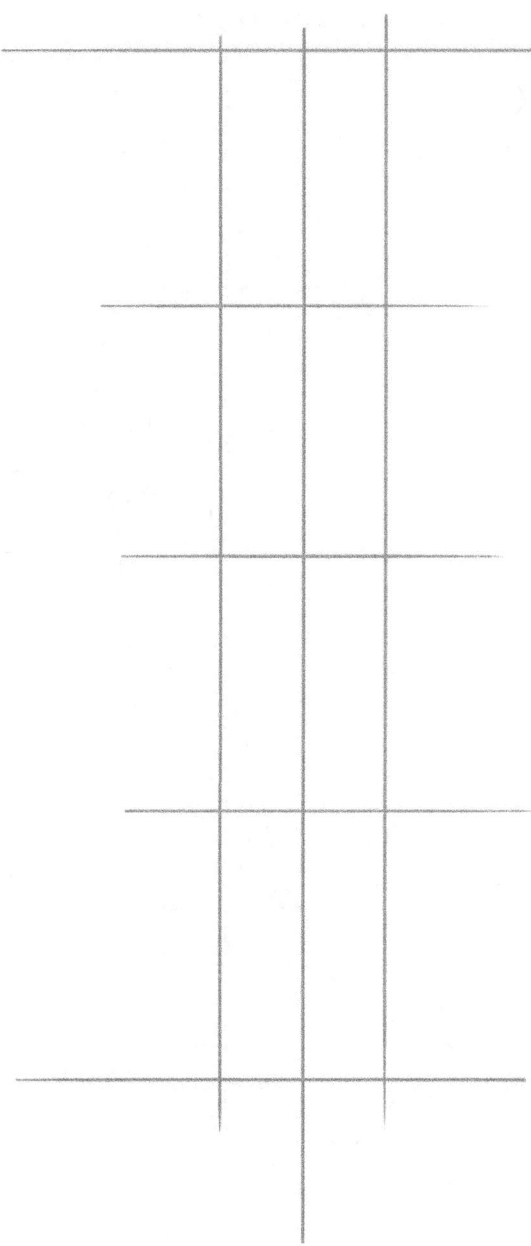

2. Using the layout for your guide, draw the lines you see in the diagram. This is the groundwork for the body and will help you flesh it out better.

sketch neck, arms and legs

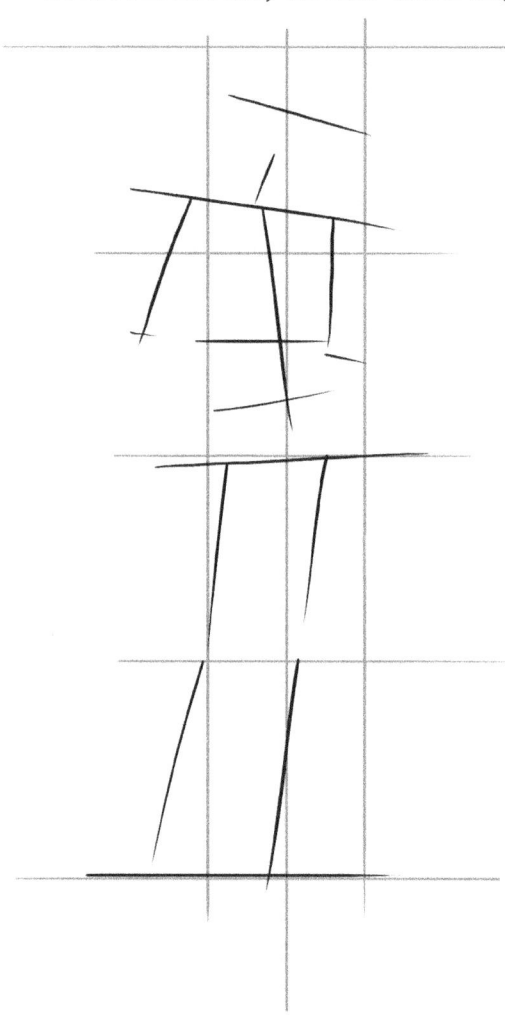

3. Draw the dome of the head.

sketch the form of head and form feet

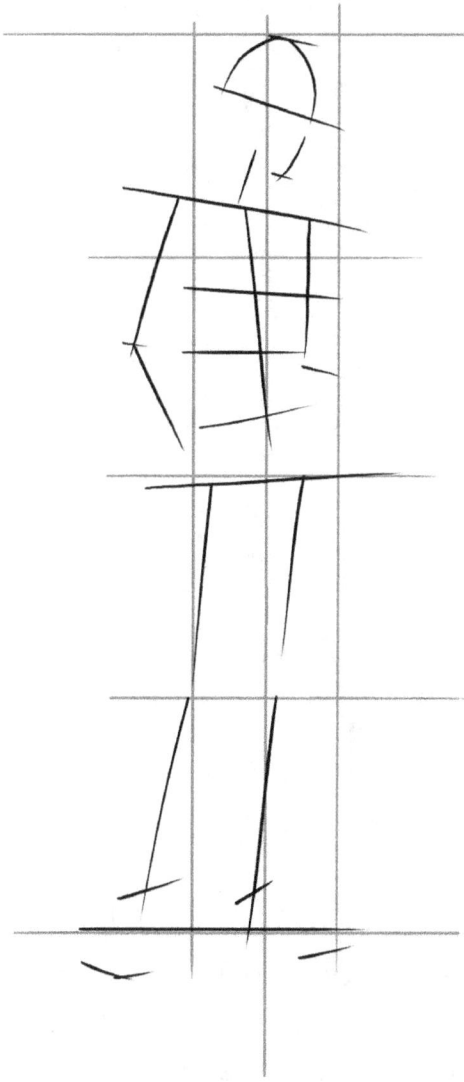

4. Add the face and chin area, remember, it's a rough sketch at this point.

5. Now, add the lines for the feet.

sketch facial features

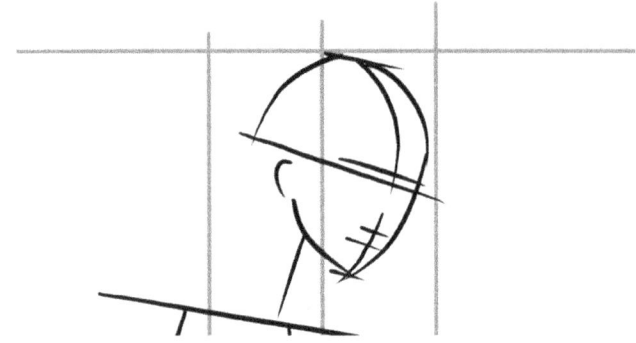

specify the form of hair

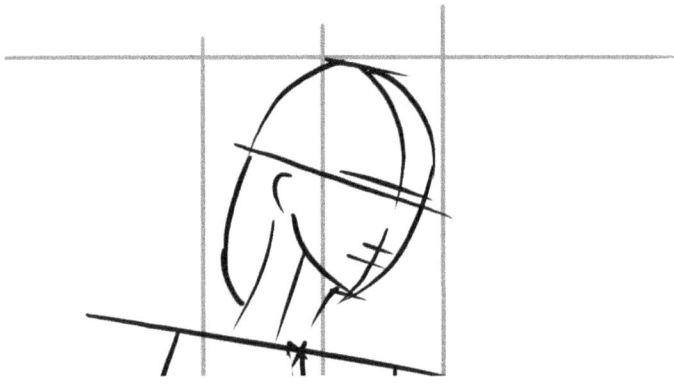

6. I've zeroed in on the face to make it easier to follow. Sketch out the rest of the face by drawing jawline first and then the dashed for the facial features.

7. Sketch in the hair.

sketch the form of breast

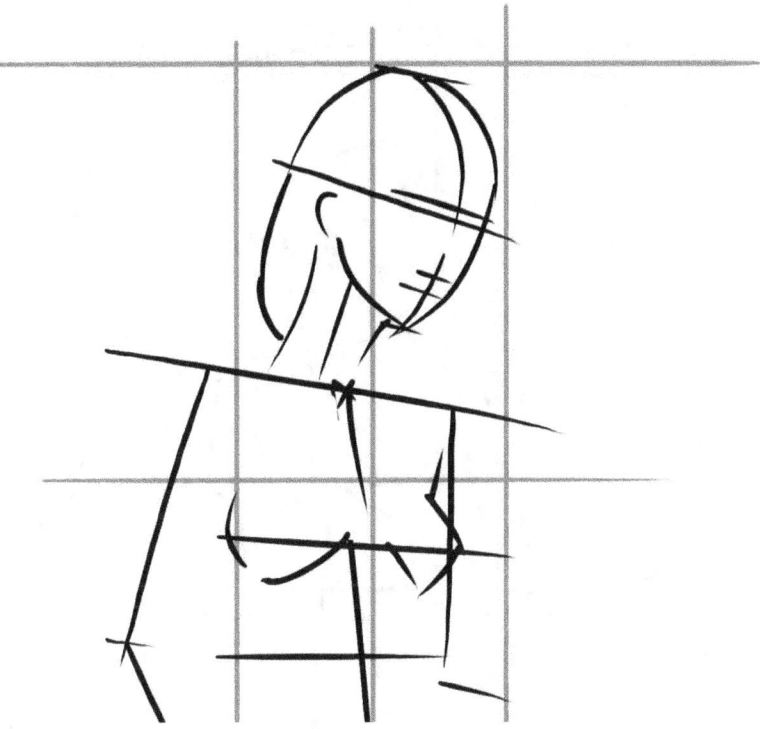

8. Using the layout, add the dashes and curves for the breasts.

9. By drawing curved lines on either side of the torso, we begin to sketch out the arms.

specify the form of arm

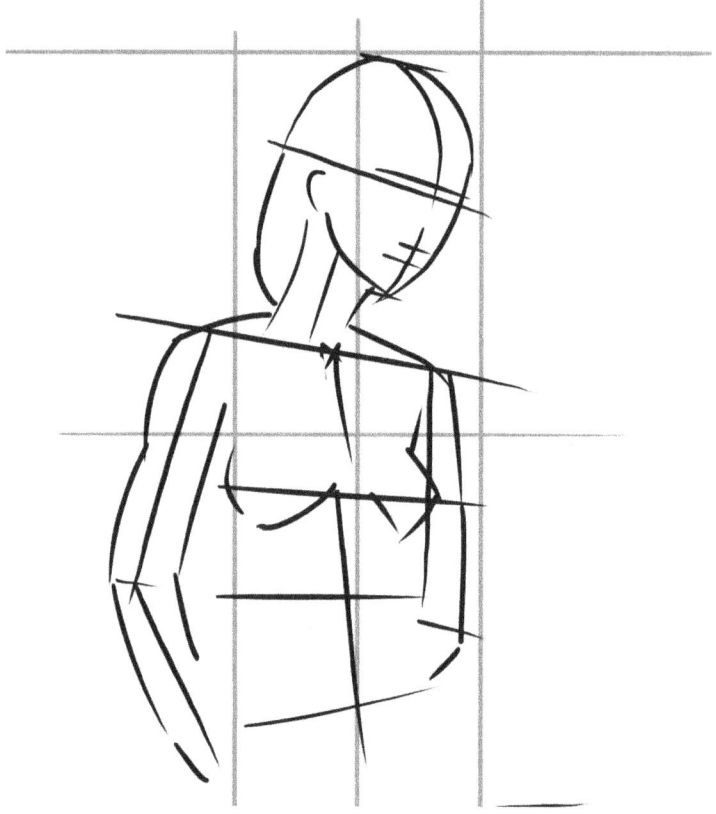

10. We're defining the muscles of the torso here.

specify the form of body

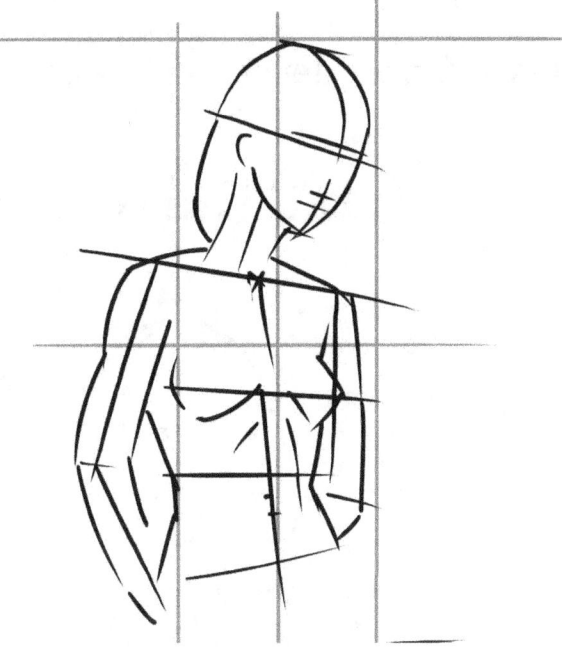

form prelum

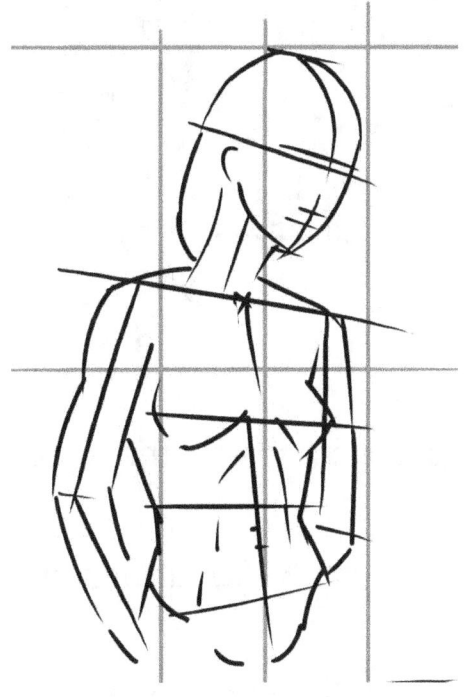

11. We are defining the hip area by making the curve before introducing the legs.

12. Add the nipples to further define the breasts.

detail the breast

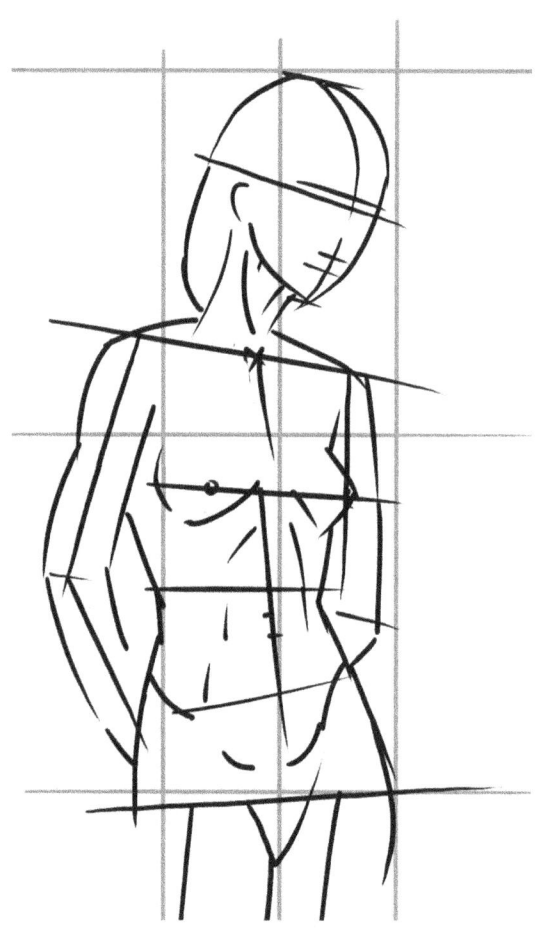

13. We are also adding the curves for the outside of the hips.

14. We are adding the curved "V" for the vaginal area.

15. Now, add the curves for the inner thighs.

sketch the form of thigh

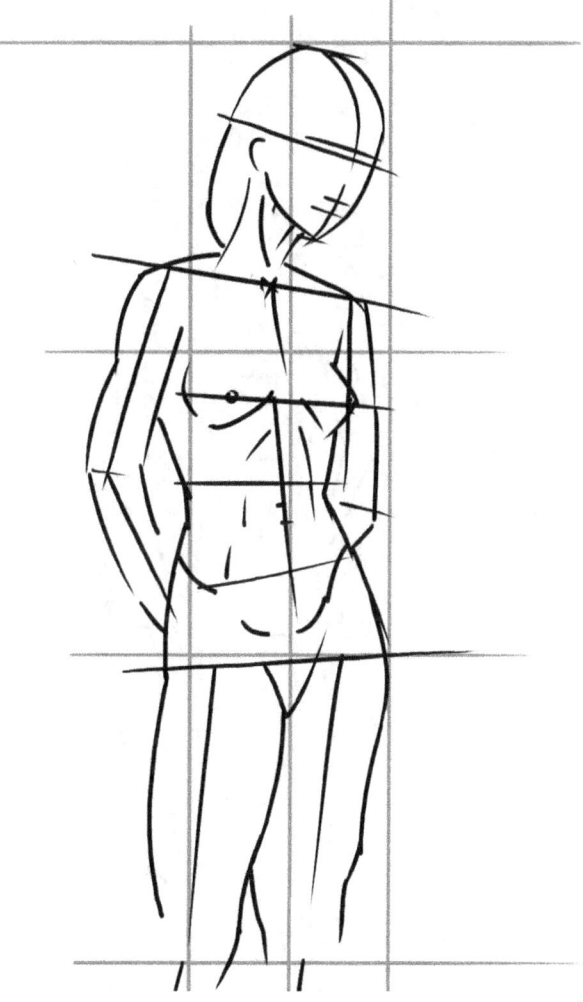

16. We're bringing the curves of the legs down, both the inner and outer portions of the legs.

form knee joint

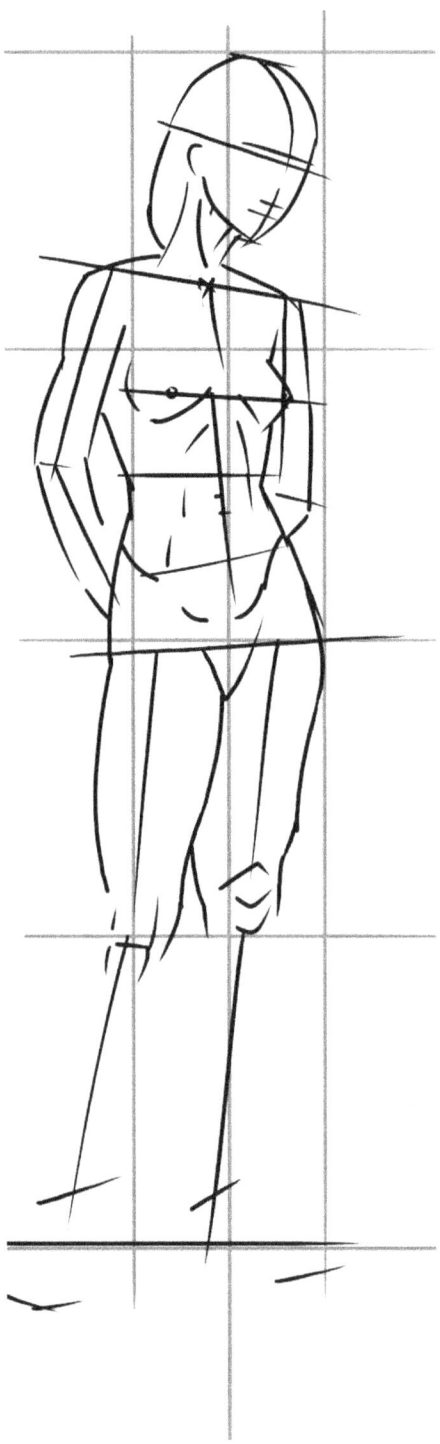

17. Starting on the right, add the slight curve for the outside of the leg.

18. Add the "V"s to outline the knees.

19. Add the lines on the inner leg.

20. The left leg has another curve to start the knee.

21. We've added half-squares for the knee in this case.

22. Add the curves for the calves of the legs. It's easier if you start from the outer part of the right leg and work your way to the outer side of the left leg.

form ankle

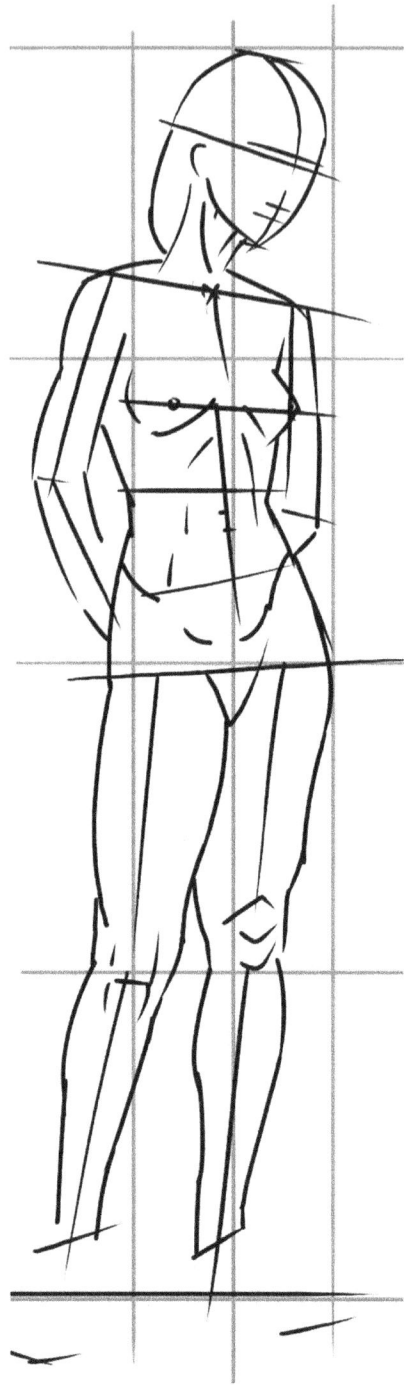

23. Start from the slant where the leg stopped and draw the back curve of the right foot.

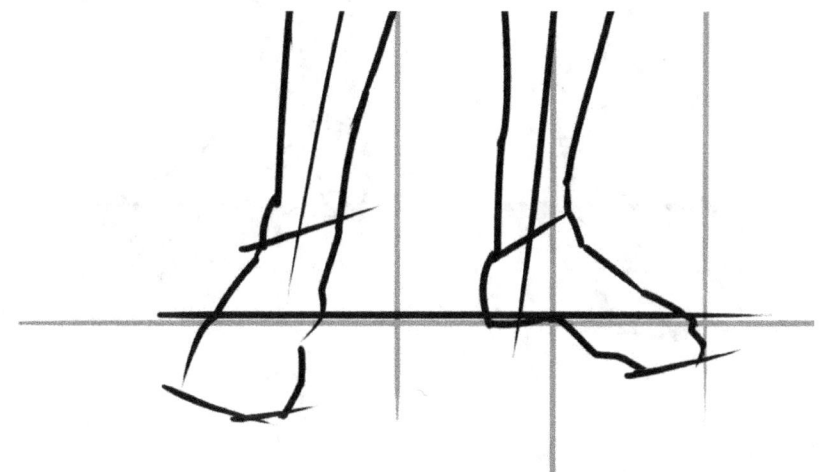

24. Now, draw the curve for the top of the foot.

25. Add the bottom of the foot.

26. Start with the inside of the left foot.

27. Round out the front of the foot.

28. Bring the curve back up to the ankle.

29. Add the lines for the toes.

30. Add the details on the tops of the feet.

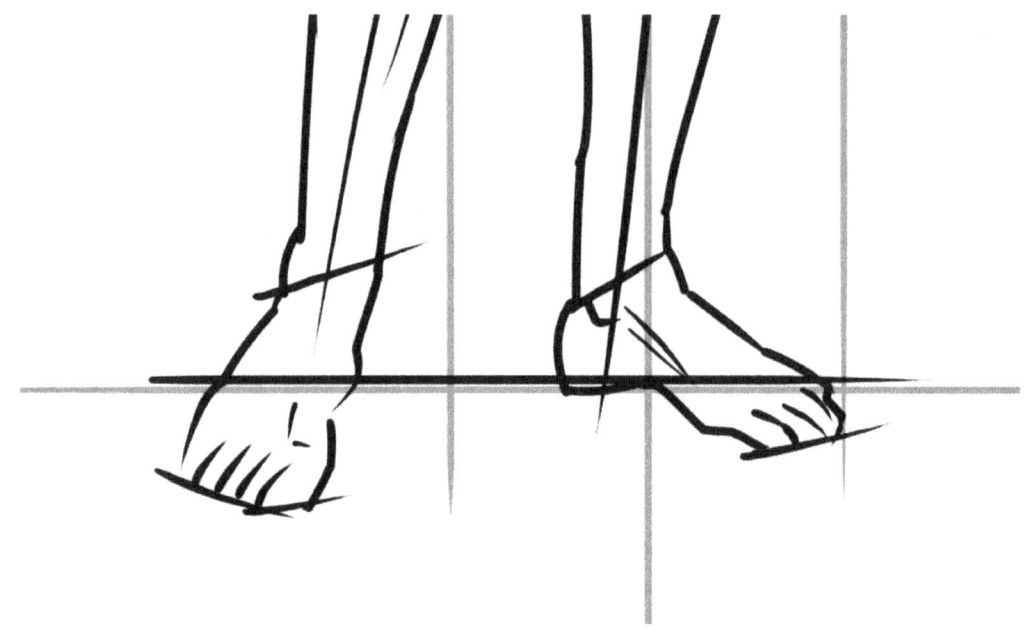

31. Add the dashes for where the eyes are going to go.

detail facial features and hand

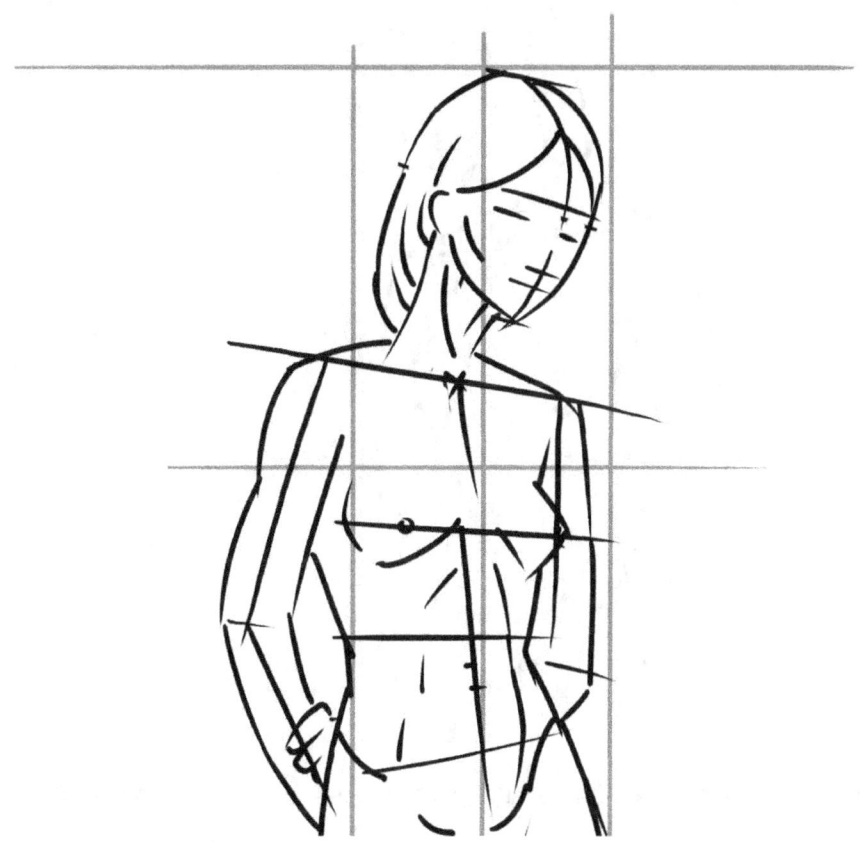

32. Define the cheekbone.

33. Add the curves for the fingers of the hand.

form collarbone

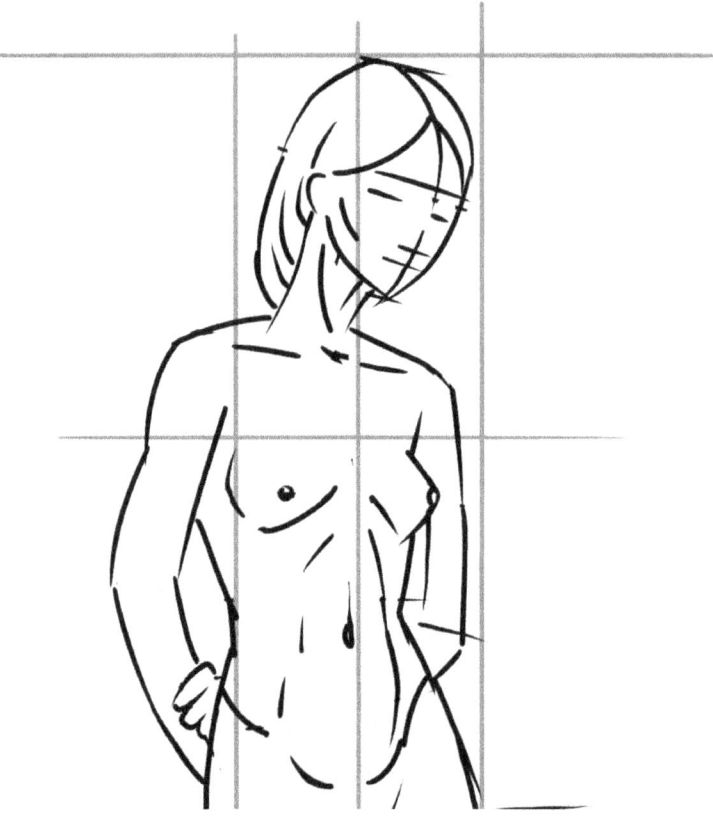

34. Clean our subject up by removing the guides for the shoulder and breast area.

35. Add the lines for the collarbone.

    Now would be a good time to compare what you've done so far with what is to the left.

36. Remove the rest of the lines we've used as a guide.

37. Add the details for the eyes. Keep in mind, the eyes here cannot look as detailed as in a previous lesson. The head is too small for that.

38. Add the nose.

39. Add the lines for the mouth.

40. Add the details for the hair.

Take one last time to look everything over before going on to the next lesson. Don't worry if it's not perfect. One does not become a master artist overnight. It takes practice, repetition, and dedication.

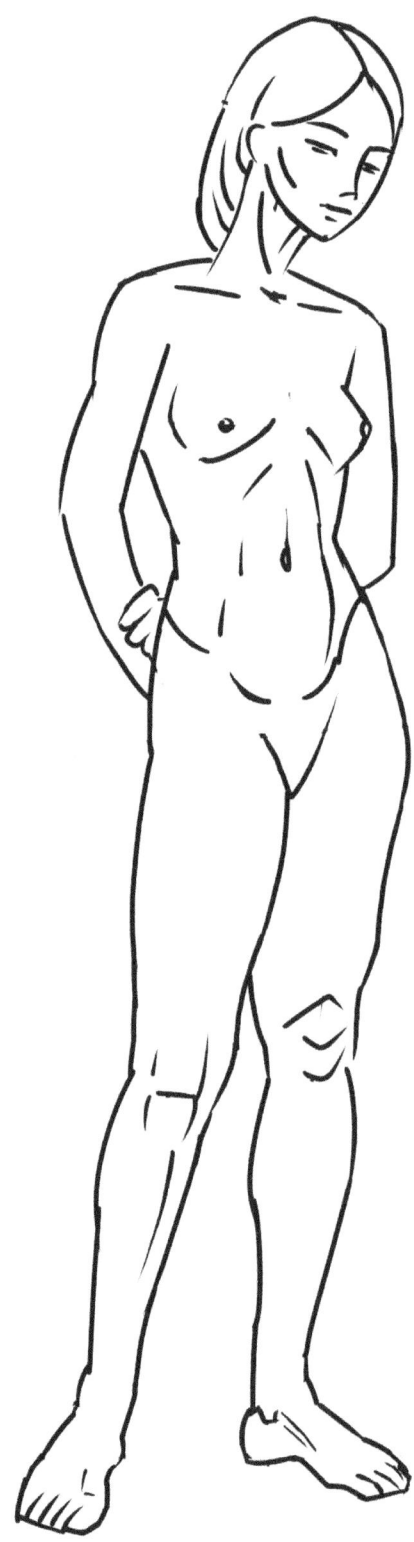

Chapter 10 - A Study of the Male Form

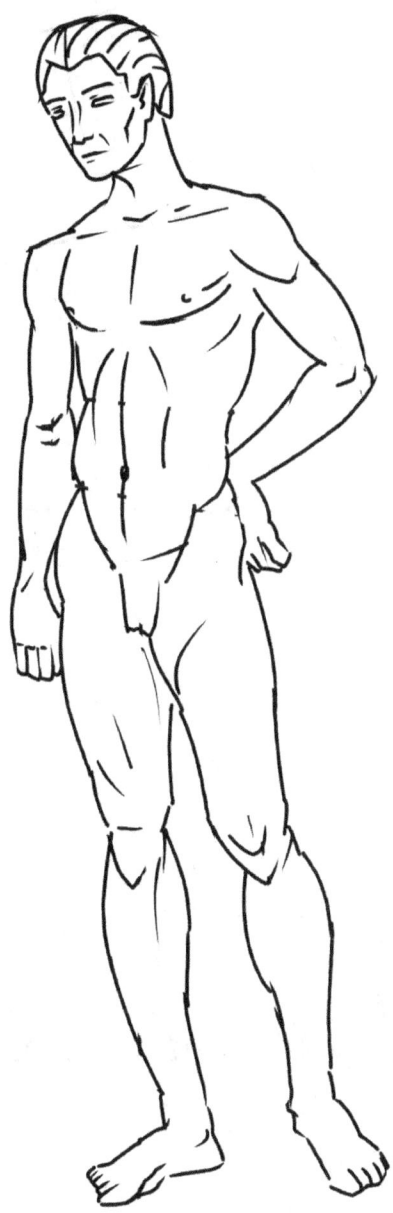

We can see, by comparing the two forms, the male figure is more blocky in appearance. This makes the male form easier to draw as a subject. Unlike the female form, the male form has delineations for the breasts and less curvature.

form layout for male figure

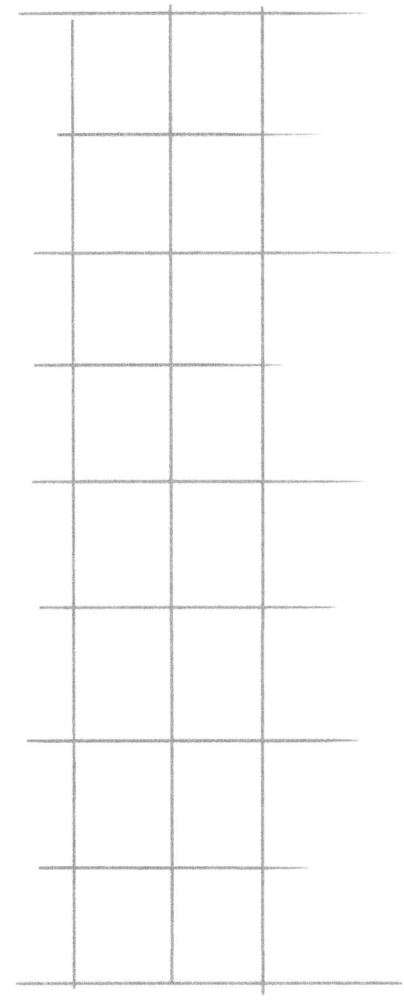

1. Start out with the layout as we did for the female figure.

sketch main construction line

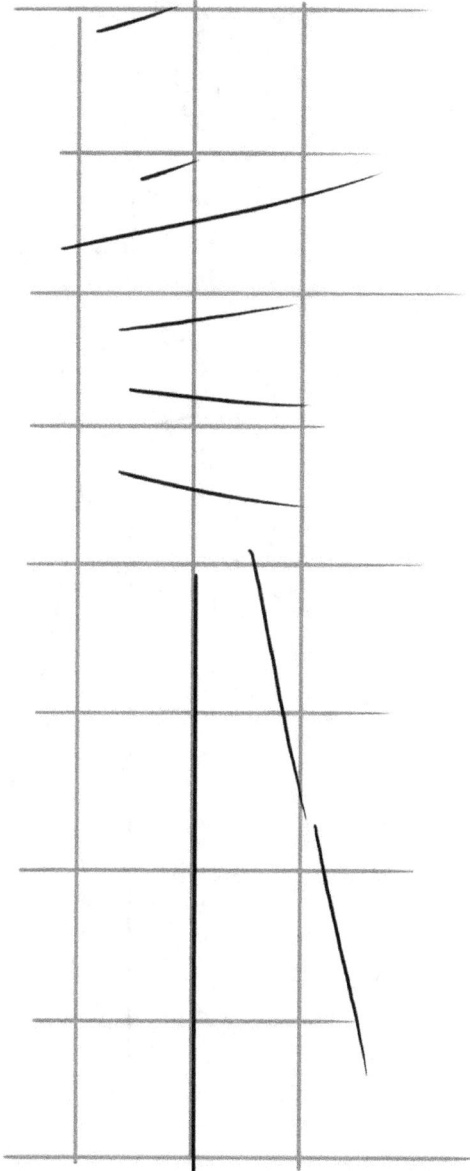

2. We now add the construction lines to help us fill in the details later.

specify facial features and feet edge

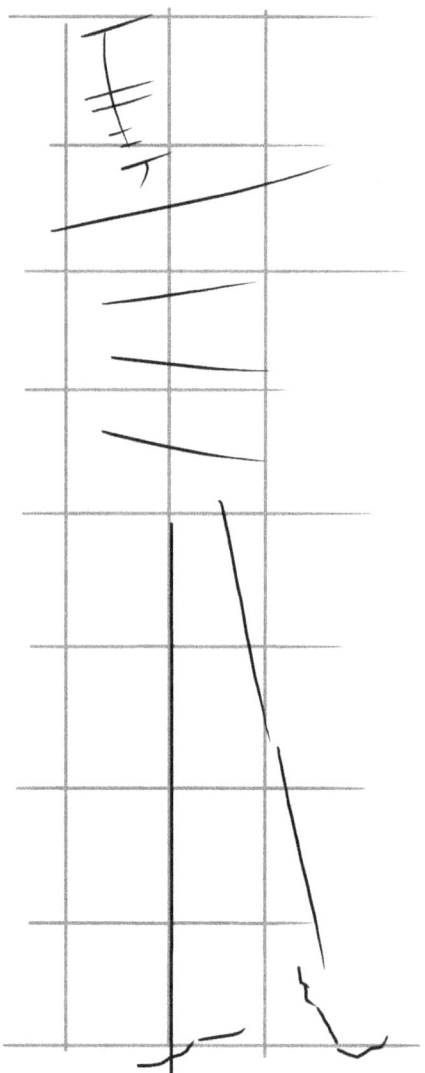

3. Add the guidelines for the face and feet.

4. Add the sketch lines for the torso.

add arms

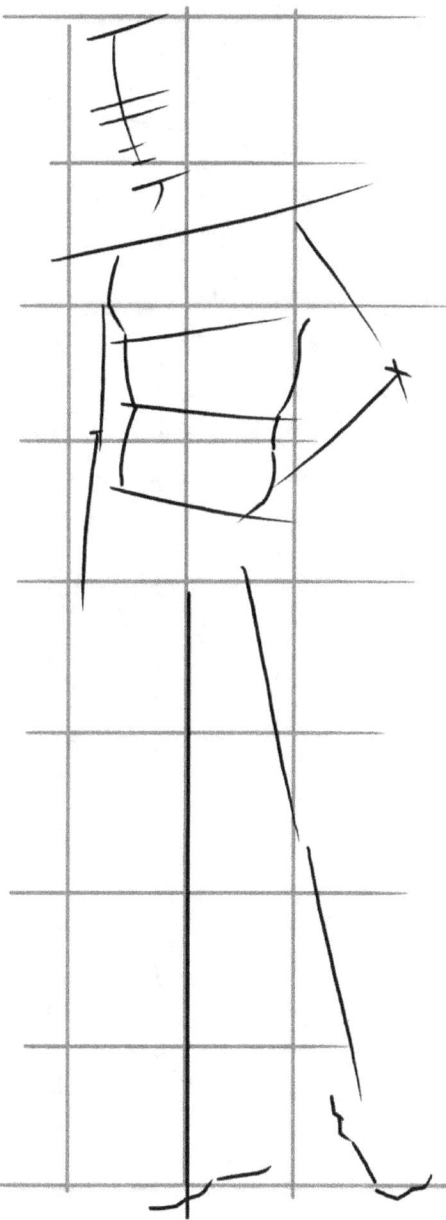

sketch body

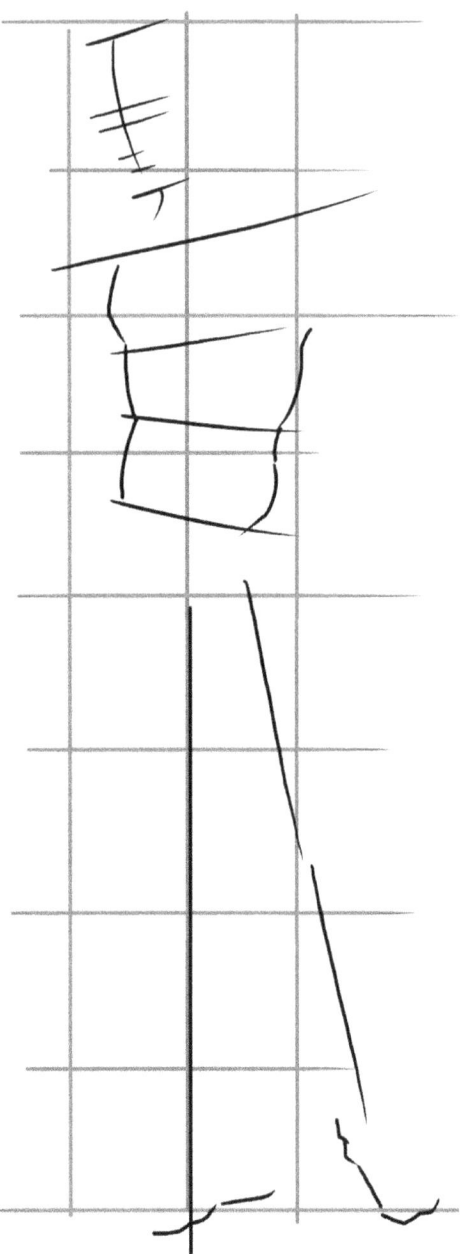

5. Add the sketch lines for the arms.

6. Now, add the lines for where the hands are going to go.

sketch prelum and intima

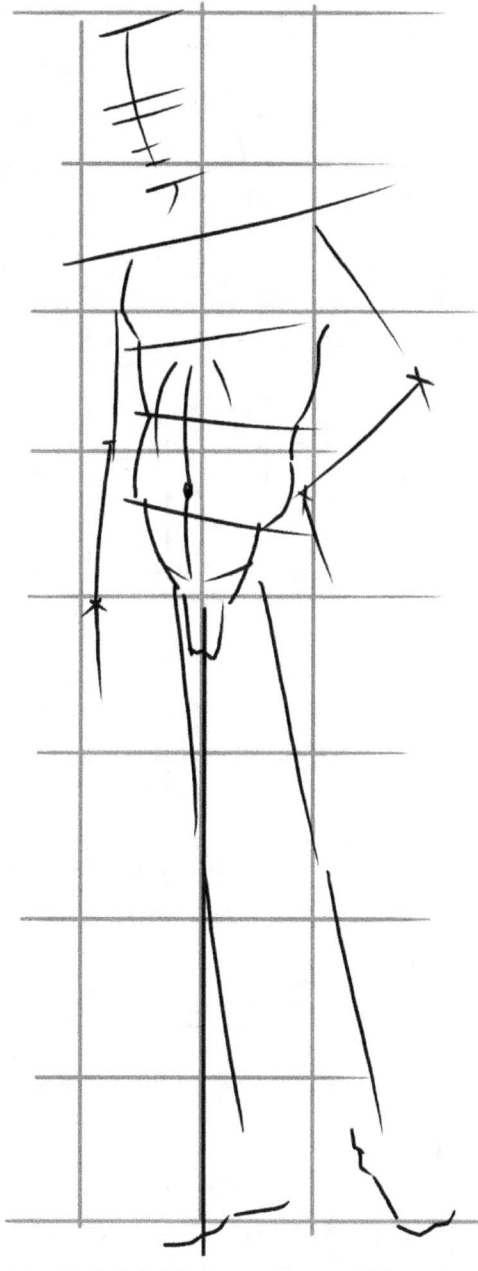

add hands

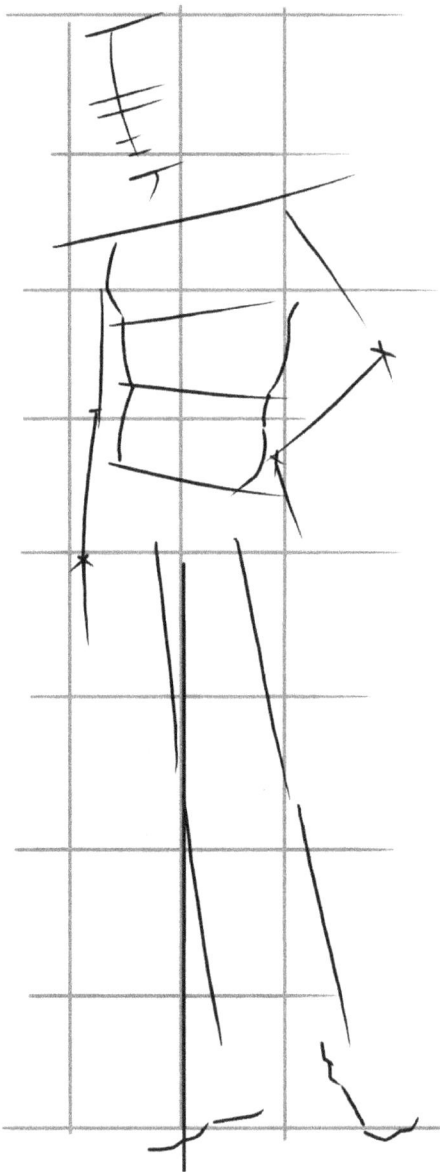

7. Starting on the left, draw the curves of the torso.

8. Do the same for the right side.

9. Now, draw the curves in the pelvic area and add the penis.

10. Define the muscles in the mid-section.

11. Don't forget the belly button.

add chest muscles

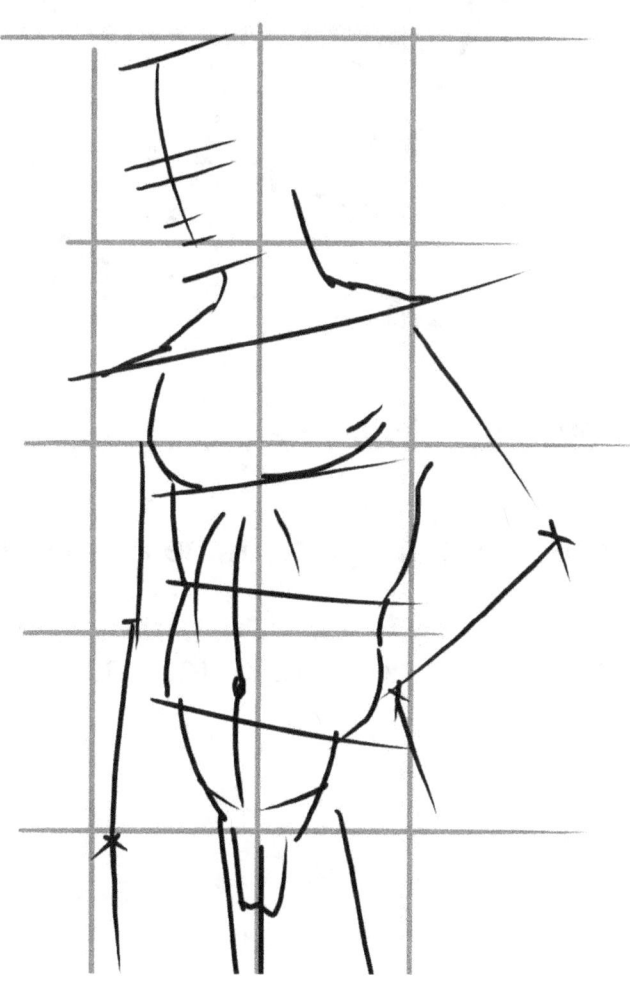

12. Add the lines for the breast area.

13. Add the curves for the neck and shoulder areas.

create brainpan

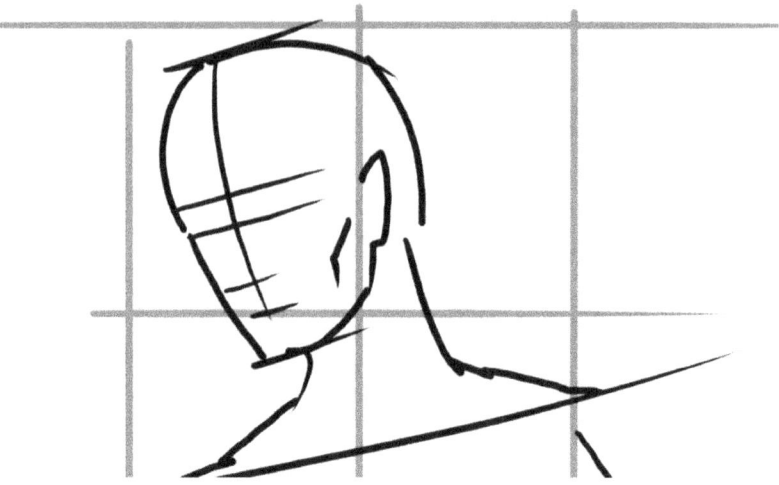

14. Draw the top of the skull first.

15. Bring the skull line down to form the edge of the face.

16. Bring the curve back up to make the chin.

add thigh and knee joint

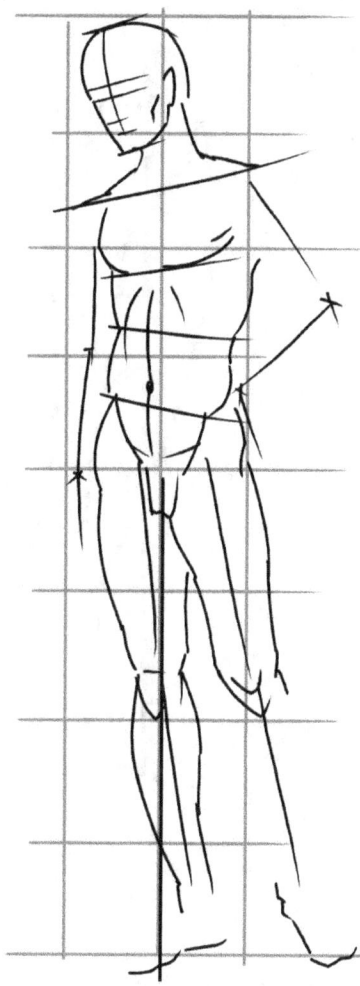

17. We're bringing the curves down out from the hip area to the thigh on the right leg first.

18. When this is finished, draw the inner thigh of the left leg.

19. Draw the outer thigh of the left leg.

20. Sketch in the lines for the knees.

21. Now, bring the lines down on the left to start the calf.

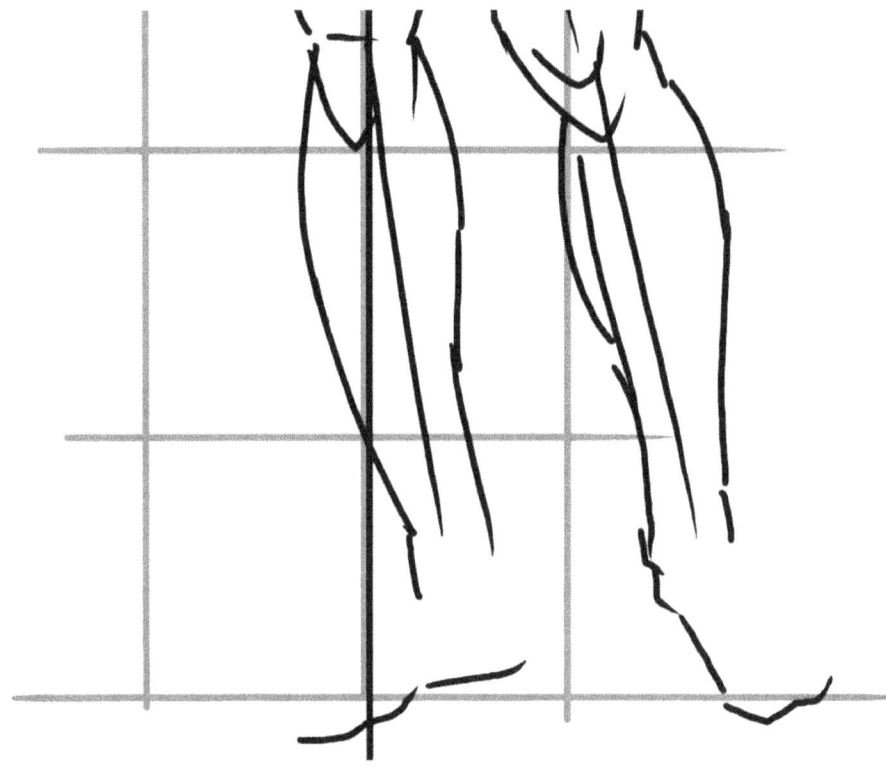

22. Bring the curve down on the right leg.

23. Now, add the ankles as you see them in the picture.

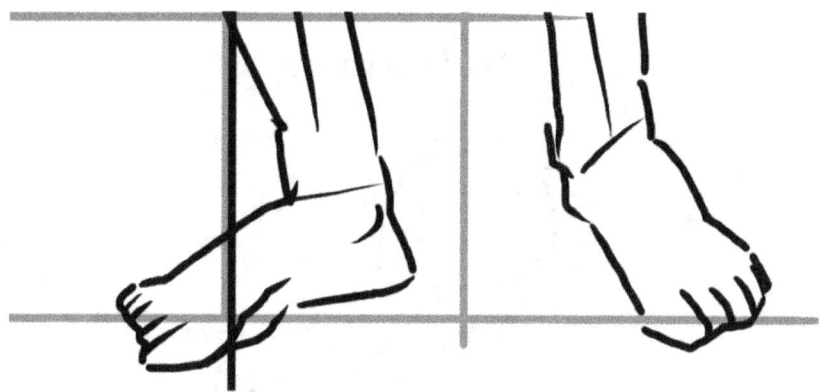

24. The next step is to finish the curves of the feet.

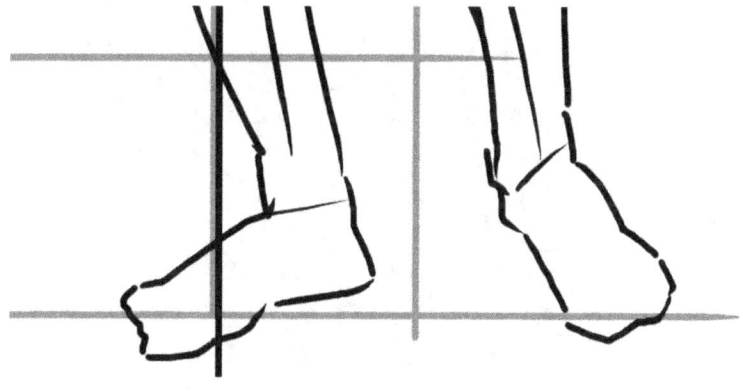

25. You can't have feet without toes. Add the small curves for the toes on each foot.

sketch arms

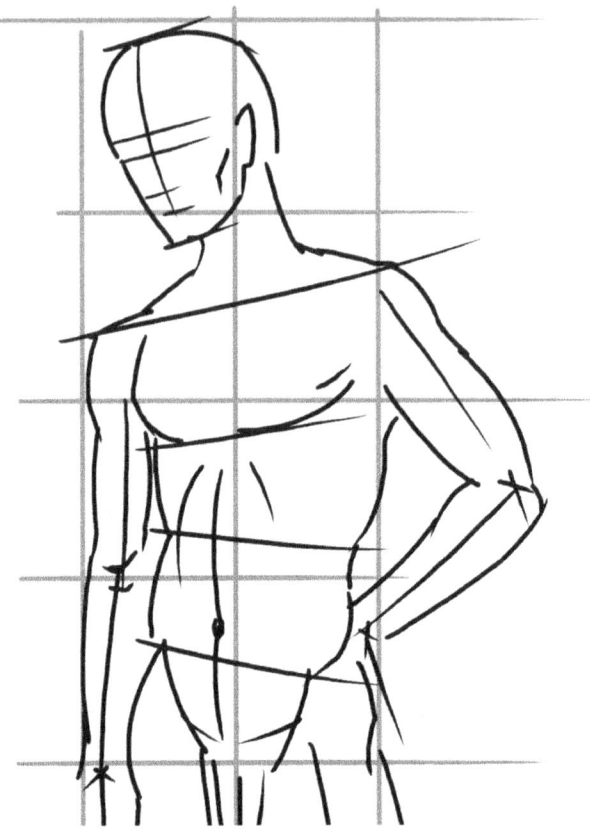

26. Following the lines you've put as guides, add the curves of the arms from the shoulder line to the elbow. Do this for both arms.

27. Now, add the lines for the forearms.

Take this time to compare your drawing the one on the left. Don't worry if it's not exact. You're still practicing.

28. After adding the arms, start on the curves for the fingers on the right hand.

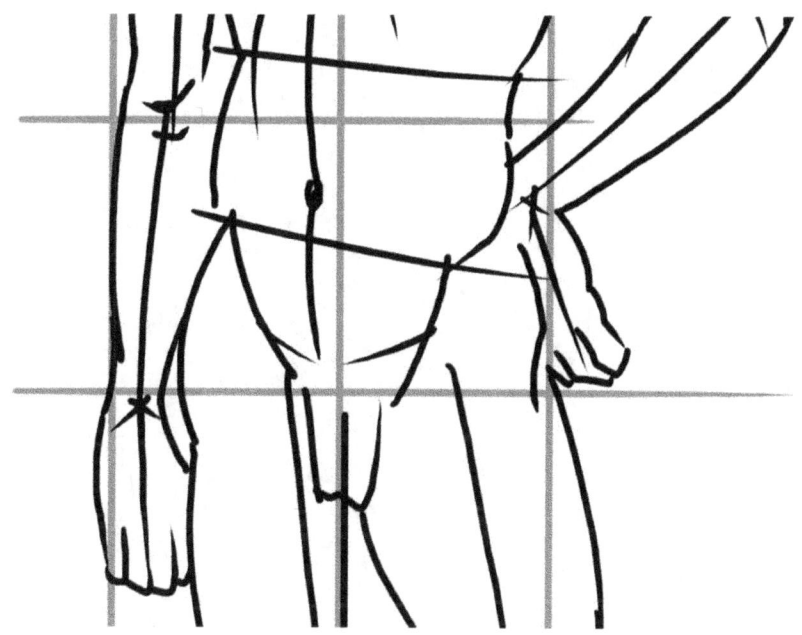

29. Draw "L" shapes for the fingers on the other hand.

specify facial features

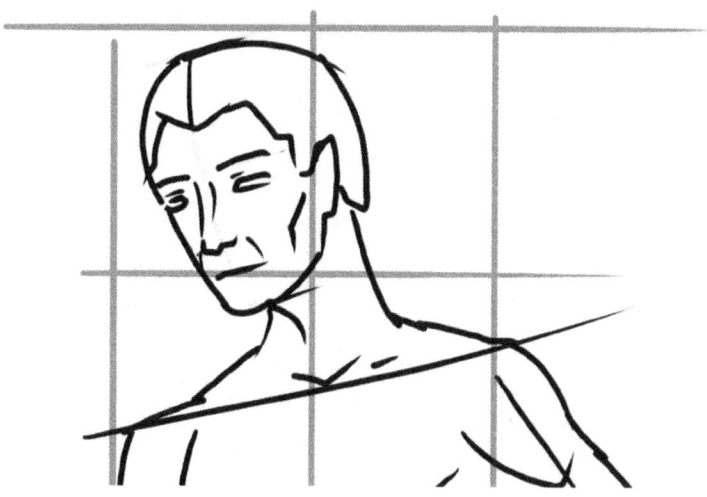

30. Add the details to the face you see to the left. Take your time. It's best to start with the eyebrows and work your way down the face.

add hair

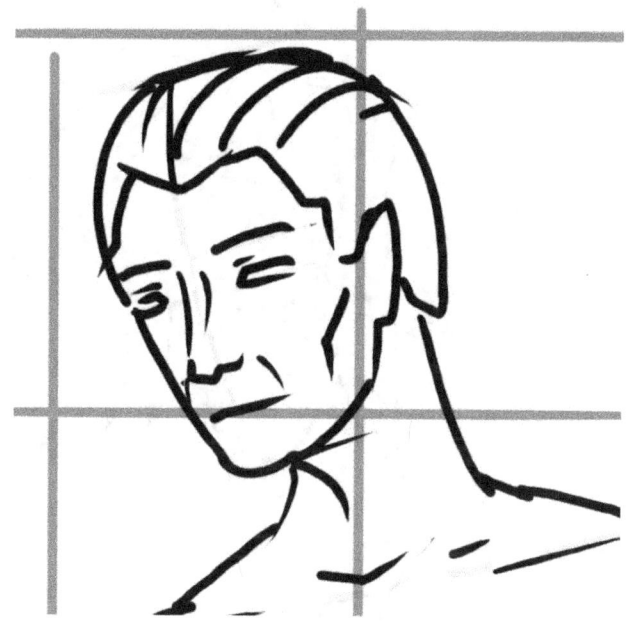

31. Slight curves tell us where the hair is.

32. Remove your lines and compare pictures.

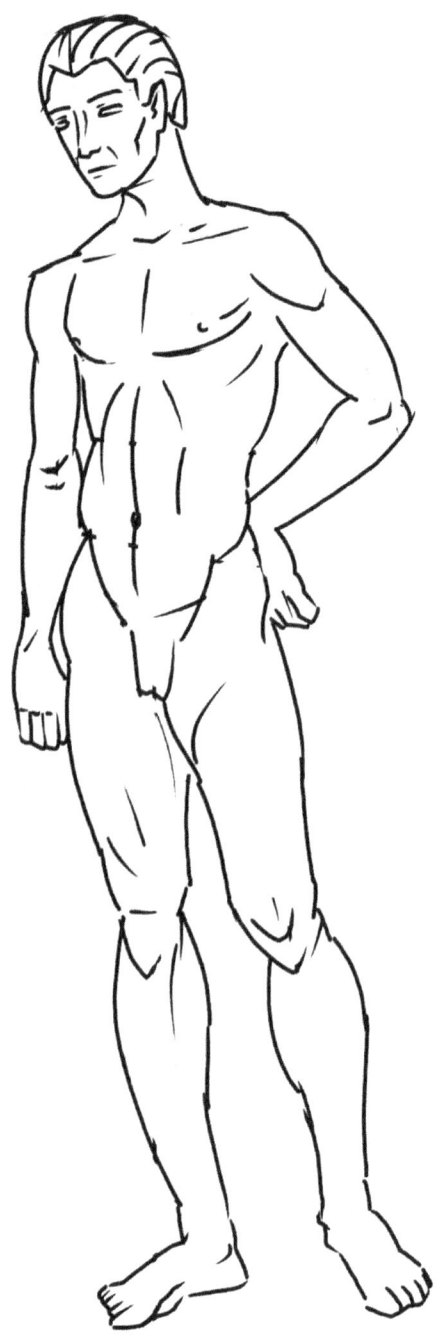

Final Words

You can go back and redo these lessons until you are comfortable with the technique. Work at your own pace and compare your recent work with your past work. Don't worry about how the other artists are doing. Everyone has their own individual style, and you will find yours with time.

I hope this books has answered you've had and even helped you improve your skill.